Ken Piesse's ABC

To every cricketer, young and old,
who shares my passion
for the greatest game of all.

Ken Piesse's ABC of Australian Cricket

A MARVELLOUS COMPENDIUM OF TALL TALES AND TRUE

echo

About the author

Ken Piesse is the most published living sports author in Australia. He has written, edited or published 85 books, including 60 on cricket – among them *Fifteen Minutes of Fame: Australia's 70 One-Test Wonders*. He is an in-demand after-dinner speaker, a keynote sports presenter for P&O and president of the Australian Cricket Society. His multimedia awards stretch from TV and radio to newspapers and magazines. Ken lives on Melbourne's famed Mornington Peninsula with his wife Susan, his swimming companion Belle and Burmese kitten Bonnie.

Foreword by Scott Boland

Six for seven.

I still shake my head in amazement. They are figures I'd have loved to produce at any of my clubs – Parkdale, the Kingston Saints and Frankston – and they came in my very first Test, in front of family and friends in my home town.

It was one of the best days of my life and the start of the best three weeks I'll probably ever have in cricket.

Just 12 months earlier, despite being in the best form of my career, I was resigned to never getting back in the Australian team. My last ODIs had been in 2016. There were just too many big names ahead of me, and all outstanding cricketers: Starc, Cummins, Hazlewood ... three of the very best fast bowlers of any generation.

Josh had hurt his side earlier in the Test series and was having a trial in Sydney. If fit, he'd play in Melbourne. I was off to one side watching every delivery, every movement. He seemed okay, but after about 10 minutes he walked across to me, smiled and said he was no good. Suddenly, I was no longer 'next cab'.

Days later, at our main pre-Test session in Melbourne, I was all over the shop. It was the worst I can remember bowling for years; I was just so nervous. Back at the team hotel Tony Dodemaide, one of the selectors, called me down from my room and said I was 'in' – I was playing.

You can imagine how I felt: 32 years of age, 80 red-ball games into my career and I was about to play my first Test.

Within half an hour of the start, I was on, from the members' end. Davey Warner walked past, grinned and said, 'Try and hit the pitch.' Gazz [Nathan Lyon] told me I'd be in an elite club if I did what he had done 10 years earlier – take a wicket with his first ball.

Though I may have looked composed on the outside, I was anything but …

The stats show that I had five overs before lunch. Apparently one was a maiden, but it all remains a blur. Paddy switched me to the far end, the Warnie end, and both Cam Green and I went around the wicket to Malan, England's number three. Walking off, I was relieved to be done with those early overs. Andrew McDonald was in the rooms and told me that I wasn't letting myself go as I normally would. He reminded me that I deserved to be out there and had nothing to lose. What's more, no-one better knew the exact, most testing 'MCG length' like me. It was reassurance I really appreciated.

England barely lasted into the final session. Taking two catches at deep midwicket off Gazz's bowling and my first Test wicket were to be a prelude to the six for seven in England's second innings.

Everything seemed to go right. At one stage I had six for five. Wow, I couldn't believe it, either! Years earlier – I was probably 14 or 15 – I got a six for nine for the Kingston Saints. But this was a Test match. And against England.

Being awarded the Mullagh Medal as the player of the match just added to my fairytale. Commentator Mark Howard said, 'Build a statue for this man.'

It was all so extraordinary … and to think a mini-lifetime earlier I'd been a 117 kilo [18½ stone] heavyweight, playing in the seconds at Frankston.

I thank 'The Master' Ken Piesse – also a Frankston boy – for allowing me to talk in print about my greatest Christmas of all. I wish him all the best with his latest cricket book.

SCOTT BOLAND
Frankston, Melbourne

Contents

Introduction

We'd just flown into Barbados and were about to join the long queue for a customs check when a big, burly security guard approached. 'You with the cricket, maan?'

'Yep.'

'Come this way,' and we waltzed through an open gate.

'Have a great time. But we're goin' to beat ya, maan.'

And they did, thanks to a classic Brian Lara 150, totally against the momentum of the game. At the height of Lara's masterful solo, even Shane Warne was bowling to seven on the boundary.

It was an epic match and, for all of us, an even more wondrous adventure. Cricket is King in Barbados. Every second vacant block seemed to have a turf cricket pitch, all rolled and ready. At Kensington Oval, Bridgetown – the pre-eminent cricket ground in the Caribbean – the food outlets were all manned by happy, smiling families, selling not only chicken and rice, but Coke, whisky and rum.

Inside the ground, I was introduced to Sir Everton Weekes. Kindly, gentle and soft-spoken, he'd been commentating on Barbados radio for decades. He'd been born in the slums, a stone's throw from the ground. Fifty years earlier, the relentless violence of his stroke play was unmatched by anyone in world cricket. I hung on his every word. And remembered to ask him for his autograph.

On the eve of that Test, a few of the fitter ones in our tour group got to bowl to the Australians at centre wicket practice. I was feeling pretty happy with myself when Justin Langer only just jammed down on my slider, zeroing in at middle and off. Michael Slater came in, defended the first and ran at the second, sending it soaring way over long-on and into the nearby market gardens. 'Think that's it for you, Master,' said Colin Miller, who was also bowling. 'That ball is not comin' back.'

The next day, within the first half an hour of the game starting, Slater danced to the third ball from the West Indian offie Nehemiah Perry and put it on top of the tin roof of the George Challenor Stand. 'Thanks Piessey,' said one of our party, 'you've played Slats into form.'

My dad loved cricket, too, and the Melbourne Cricket Ground was a home away from home for us both. We'd attend all the major matches: Sheffield Shield, tour matches and Tests, me always on his Ladies Ticket. I'd score the games ball-by-ball and I still have my much-thumbed NSW Junior Cricket Union scorebooks, which include Jack Potter's wondrous 221 in the Christmas 'test' against New South Wales and, a year or so later, Garth McKenzie's 'six-for', all before lunch against the Indians. I still recall the unmistakeable roar for a fall of a wicket later that game. Ajit Wadekar was out for 99 and we were still outside queueing.

One Christmas he bought me the 1965 *Wisden* and I memorised most of it, page by page, marvelling, in particular, at the feats of Bobby Simpson and Peter Burge, who started one Shield season with massive scores of 359 and 283.

I borrowed all 18 cricket books from our local library at Parkdale in Melbourne and sat them in a new bookcase I'd made at woodwork class, imagining they were all mine.

Many a night I'd wait for Dad to come home from work. 'Can you leave the car out in the street please?' It was the signal for him to take off his suit jacket and bowl five minutes of his Scotch College offies to me in our carport. He had a bung knee from jumping out of a plane during the war. And an artificial eye, which had a habit of mischievously popping out just when it was his best mate's shout.

Dinner-table conversation centred around sport: cricket and the Hawthorn FC. At dinner one night, my sister Anne was asked to 'pass the Bill Lawry'. Unerringly, she reached for the bottle opener. Brother Jim, a drummer, was at a gig when he was told to 'use the Ashleys'. Without hesitation, he grabbed a pair of mallets.

Years earlier, when they were building our family house in Beaumaris, Dad asked Mum to find out the cricket score. Mum came back with a cuppa and proudly announced how someone was just out: 'caught in Bedser's leg trap'.

'And what is that, Patty?'

'I've got no idea!'

Mum was at a home game one Saturday at St Bede's. I was opening up and just as the bowler was delivering his first ball, she moved directly behind his arm – and into my eyeline – 'to get a better view', as she was to explain later. Luckily for me it was wide. Calling to our club umpire, I said, 'Chopper, can you ask that young lady to go back to mid-off please!'

Another time at St Bede's, a left-hander slogged me over the high cyclone fence at cow corner. The ball landed on Beach Road in front of the old Mentone hotel. A fella in a sports car saw the ball in the middle of the road, stopped, pocketed it and drove off laughing.

Cricket has always been a full-time companion. I've been fortunate to watch and comment on Tests around the world from Cape Town to Christchurch and Leeds to Lord's, to Bridgetown and beyond.

We were at rowdy Edgbaston the momentous early August week when Australia stormed back into a Test it had no right to win, thanks to the heroics of Shane Warne – with ball and bat – and a gripping last-wicket stand from Brett Lee and Michael Kasprowicz. Somehow, between strains of The Turtles and their iconic hit 'So Happy Together', Australia edged to within a boundary of a remarkable comeback win, before Kasper was caught behind.

Andrew Kuuse at Sport 927 crossed to me seven or eight times that tumultuous Sunday for live on-air updates. 'Why is Andrew ringing so often?' my wife Susan asked.

'Let him. It's Sunday night back home … he's bringing us luck.'

It was my 50th birthday and that morning we'd put 50 quid on Australia winning at most generous odds. It would have been one heck of a party. Well, it was, anyway.

Being able to share so many of my stories has always been a joy. If someone has played cricket, no matter when or where, I want to know more.

At an Over 60s game just recently, I tried to hit a finger spinner over the old Frankston Tip, missed and there was a stumping appeal. My back foot was down, but we all looked around to the elderly square leg umpire and there was no-one there! He'd gone AWOL … to have a leak.

The scope and scale of cricket's best and most riveting yarns are endless. For every Smith, Starc and Cummins, there are hundreds of others with a story to tell.

I've stood at the top of the hill leading down to Wingello Oval's concrete wicket, imagining Bill O'Reilly eyeing the emerging Bowral wizard Don Bradman decades earlier. Tiger bowled the young Don with his very first ball that mid-January Saturday in 1926. The only problem for Tiger was that it was a two-day game and the previous weekend, in Bowral, Bradman had started the match with 234 not out!

Many fellow cricket buffs and aficionados have generously assisted me in this quirky miscellany of fun, facts, oddities and anecdotes. I'm particularly grateful for the contributions from Dave Breheny, Peter Bedford, Mark Browning, Colin Clowes, Charles Davis, Ric Finlay, Lyall Gardner, Paul Harvey, Alf James, Simon McEvoy, Geoff Poulter and Geoff Sando; thanks also to my publishers Echo/Bonnier for their faith, and for their introduction to expert designer Josh.

And to my wife Susan, of course, for being so indulgent of my 24/7 hobby and allowing me the time to develop this, my latest and 65th cricket book.

KEN PIESSE
Mt Eliza, Melbourne

a'Beckett to Austin

Ted a'Beckett senior The St Kilda allrounder's somersaulting catch low down at silly mid-on to dismiss Jack Hobbs at Headingley was the catch of the 1930 Ashes summer.

Rod Adkins Wanting to leave early to attend a mate's wedding, Rod opened the batting for Nerrana, scored a century, doubled it up and went all the way to 307, batting the entire afternoon: Leongatha, Victoria, 1998–99. He missed the service but made the reception.

Terry Alderman Dislocated his shoulder and missed a year's cricket after falling heavily while tackling a spectator who had run onto the WACA Ground: First Ashes Test, Perth, November 1982.

Harry Alexander Went AWOL during a Sheffield Shield match to lay a bet at the Caulfield races and forfeited his batting place at number 11 after a Victorian collapse against New South Wales: Melbourne, December 1931.

All out for 0 Walcha Under 16s vs the Armidale School, Armidale, NSW, 1972. (The Walcha Show was on that weekend and only five of the locals made it to the bus in time. Walcha improved in its second innings, making 13, but lost by an innings.)

Spring Creek also made 0 against Headingley Hill in country Queensland in 1933–34. All 11 players batted.

The first known instance of a team being dismissed without scoring occurred at Moore Park in Sydney in 1876 when Marlborough was out for 0 against Undaunted.

All out in under six overs Penrith's First XI at Springwood, Nepean District, NSW, December 1983. The team made 12 from 34 balls, with seven players failing to score.

Frank Allan Dubbed the 'Bowler of the Century', the rangy left-arm swerve bowler declined an invitation to play in the very first Test match in Melbourne to meet friends at the Warrnambool Agricultural Show. Later became Victoria's Chief Inspector for Vermin.

Bill Alley Scored twin centuries, aged 42, against Richie Benaud's 1961 touring Australians. Released his autobiography *Standing the Test of Time*, aged 80, in 1999.

Sam Anderson Tall and athletic, from the Wakka Wakka nation near Ipswich, Queensland, Sam scored an estimated 100 career centuries – five came in one season on the NSW north coast at Casino in 1913–14 and nine in Lismore in 1919–20. Known as the Prince of Darkness, he was a one-man cricket team, a champion batsman, bowler and wicketkeeper. He once caught Don Bradman for a duck. Highest of his numerous century opening stands with fellow Indigenous player Alex James was 304 for Bungawalbyn against Greenridge in 1913–14.

Confident in his own abilities, from controlling a team of bullocks to swinging an axe, he was the champion of north Queensland. Once, when he and James were walking out to bat, he called to his captain, 'Who comes in after Alex?'

He had his own trick shot, a flick to fine leg between his legs. The respect for him bordered on awe.

He trialled in Sydney, but was homesick and stayed only briefly.

His recorded run sprees on the far north coast occurred when he was in his early thirties. Little is known of his feats in his twenties.

Still playing at 70, he was in Lismore one day watching Freddie Brown's English cricket team practise prematch at an otherwise deserted Oakes Oval when Brown, told of Anderson's cricketing achievements, walked up and introduced himself and asked if Sam would like a hit. Years later, Sam quipped: 'I finally got to play a game against the Poms.'

Tommy Andrews Responsible for one of the great between-the-wars Ashes catches with a one-hander at silly point after Patsy Hendren, on 0, crunched an Arthur Mailey full toss out of the screws: Leeds, UK, July 1926.

Had 30 seasons and scored 28 centuries at Petersham, NSW, where the scoreboard is named in his honour. A stonemason by trade, Andrews made the headstones for Victor Trumper and Archie Jackson.

Jo Angel The first West Australian to 400 Sheffield Shield wickets.

Denise Annetts Known as Little One (she's only 154 centimetres – just over five foot), her career Test average of 81 is second only to Don Bradman.

Peggie Antonio The diminutive 1930s wrist spinner was known as The Girl Grimmett. She was just 153 centimetres (five foot) tall.

George Arcadiou The son of a Greek panel-beater, he is the first known 16-year-old to score a quadruple century: Druids vs North Sunshine, Melbourne 1967–68.

Ron Archer Was being groomed for the Australian captaincy before badly twisting his knee in a one-off matting Test at Karachi in 1956. Attempted a comeback but was never as good.

Harry Armstrong Umpired the Australia–West Indies Sydney Test in February 1931, after only three previous first-class matches – the shortest umpiring 'apprenticeship' on record.

Warwick Armstrong Australia's heaviest Test captain at 133 kilograms (21 stone), Armstrong was known as The Big Ship and was considered as immovable at the crease as Adelaide Oval's Moreton Bay fig trees. His tent-like shirt and huge boots are a feature of the MCC's museum.

Mickey Arthur Was sacked as Australia's head coach just days into the 2013 Ashes tour. Had won 10 of his 19 Tests in charge. A disastrous earlier campaign to India was costly. At Mohali, he wrote his own death warrant by insisting that four players be stood down from the Test match for not completing a homework assignment.

Ossie Asher The only batsman in NSW representative history to make a century from the number 11 spot: NSW Second XI vs Victoria Second XI, Melbourne, 1921–22.

Max Atwell Tasmania's number one cricket bibliophile, his array of cricket books and annuals was purchased by

Cricket Tasmania (CT) and now forms the nucleus of an imposing collection housed, initially, in the boardroom of the AGC Pavilion at Bellerive before becoming the centrepiece of CT's magnificent museum.

Harold Austin Once clubbed a ball over the old Arden Street grandstand and into an adjoining paddock: North Melbourne Cricket Ground, 1929–30.

ADELAIDE OVAL HAPPENINGS

NOVEMBER 2015

Batting with a broken foot, Mitchell Starc hobbles, rather than sprints, the winning runs in a gripping finale to the first-ever floodlit pink-ball trans-Tasman Test. He misses the rest of the summer. Set 187, Australia loses seven wickets in the chase, a damning earlier error by third umpire Nigel Llong pivotal in NZ's defeat.

NOVEMBER 2012

On his way to an imperious 224 not out by stumps, Michael Clarke hits five fours from one over from South Africa's Morne Morkel. The first is dispatched over extra cover, and the others through point, behind point, straight mid-off and the final one, straight back past the bowler.

DECEMBER 1972

Rod Marsh is bowled after attempting the first-ever reverse sweep by an Australian Test batsman. He'd made 118, the first Test century ever by an Australian wicketkeeper.

THE ASHES

Ashes battles are likened to war without weapons. Often the niceties of yesteryear are forgotten or flaunted. In Brisbane in 2013–14, so furious was Australia's captain Michael Clarke at the sledging English player Jimmy Anderson reserved for first-game Tasmanian George Bailey that he said, 'Get ready to get your fuckin' arm broken.'

...

Seeing Australia reach 600 on the third morning of the 1964 Old Trafford Test, one disgruntled Lancastrian spectator turned to the Australian balcony and boomed, 'Declare, Simpson, you bastard!' Wicketkeeper Wally Grout immediately countered with: 'What about The Oval '38?' referencing England's seven for 903 declared, still the highest score in Ashes history.

...

As Andrew Symonds walked into bat in the Christmas Ashes Test in Melbourne in 2006, Kevin Pietersen called, 'Here comes the specialist fielder.' Averaging just 18 before the match, Symonds made a Test-best 156, including a straight six to bring up his maiden Test hundred.

...

Had Australia's deputy captain Vic Richardson had his way in 1932–33, Bodyline would have been unleashed by both teams. Vic never shied away from a fight and when Douglas Jardine, England's captain, knocked on the dressing room door with a grievance one day, Vic asked his team, 'Which one of you bastards called this bastard a bastard?'

... The Ashes continued

Terry Alderman's triumphant comeback into Ashes cricket in 1989 saw him take 41 wickets, including 19 leg before wicket. Graham Gooch fell lbw five times in the series and recorded a message on his answering machine: 'I'm out at the moment: lbw Alderman.'

...

In 2009, the Barmy Army climbed into a wayward, out-of-sync Mitch Johnson, chorusing: 'He bowls to the left, he bowls to the right; that Mitchell Johnson ... he bowls a lot of shite.'

...

The plaudits for England's victorious 2005 Ashes squad included MBEs for everyone, from Her Majesty the Queen. Even Paul Collingwood was recognised, despite playing only once, in the final Test at The Oval, where he scored seven and 10. Just over 12 months afterwards, Collingwood, a likeable and gritty player, was taking guard during the opening Test at the Gabba in Brisbane. Ignoring the pitch microphones, slips fielder Shane Warne was at his most colourful: 'You got an MBE, right? For 7 ... SEVEN. How embarrassing is that?'

...

When Leicestershire's bowling allrounder Jimmy Ormond was a late addition to England's XI for the final Test in 2001, he was marking guard when Mark Waugh, from slip, interrupted: 'Mate, what the fuck are you doing out here? There's no way you're good enough to play for England.'

'At least I'm the best player in my family,' replied Ormond.

Badcock to Bushfire

Jack Badcock The Tasmanian Bradman.

Kevin Badcock Had his jaw broken by a thunderous Viv Richards straight drive, hit with such ferocious power that Badcock didn't have time to even raise his hands to protect himself: Tasmania vs Queensland, Brisbane, December 1976.

Ken Baillie Reached the phenomenal milestone of 1000 Adelaide Country Week wickets in 1962, aged 48. From Tumby Bay on the Eyre Peninsula, he once had Don Bradman stumped in a pre-war game at Kadina.

Darrel Baldock The champion Aussie Rules footballer of the '60s and '70s, he made a half century against the touring West Indies: Launceston, January 1961.

Cameron Bancroft Co-instigator of Cape Town's shameful sandpaper scandal which triggered a stream of resignations, suspensions and brought Australian cricket to its knees in March 2018.

Alick Bannerman The noted nineteenth century stonewaller once took umbrage at a teammate singing music hall ditties in the slips. 'My friend, we are playing cricket,' he said.

Eric Barbour Sydney's greatest schoolboy cricketer. In the 1908–09 season alone, he made 2146 runs and took 142 wickets, including 356 and 11 wickets for the match for Sydney Grammar against Shore, North Sydney.

Warren Bardsley Australia's oldest captain, he deputised, aged 43, for Herbie Collins in the Headingley and Old Trafford Tests in 1926. He attributed his longevity, in part, to not drinking, smoking or eating meat.

Sid Barnes Once jumped the MCC members' turnstiles to gain entry on a Test match morning, having given away his player's ticket to a mate. Years earlier he'd taken 40 runs from a nine-ball over from Ginty Lush: Petersham vs North Sydney, 1936–37. Was barred from a Test comeback for 'reasons other than cricket'.

Ben Barnett His distinguished contributions to the game spanned four decades, but often centre around the moment he missed stumping Len Hutton, on 40, at The Oval, London, in 1938. Hutton went on to make the new world-record solo score of 364.

Dr John Barrett The first to carry his bat in an Ashes Test: Lord's, July 1890.

Edmund Barton Australia's first prime minister umpired five NSW vs Victoria intercolonial matches in the mid-1870s. He also officiated at the Sydney 'Riot' in 1879, when several English players were attacked by invading members of the crowd.

Carl Bashford Took all 20 wickets in a bush match in Victoria in 1904. *See* Lou Benaud

Bay 13 A hub for the noisiest and thirstiest supporters at the Melbourne Cricket Ground in the '70s and '80s.

David Beck Saved a 13-year-old Shane Warne from drowning after Warne knocked himself out when jumping off the pier at his local beach, Half Moon Bay in Black Rock, 25 minutes south of Melbourne's CBD. Seeing Warne motionless and floating face down in the shallows, Beck jumped in and hauled him back to shore.

Martin Bedkober Died, aged 22, when struck over the heart during a Brisbane First XI club match at Toombul, December 1975. As a schoolboy prodigy, he'd broken Bobby Simpson's Petersham–Marrickville record, with 645 runs in the AW Green Shield Under 16 competition in 1968–69.

Eric Beecher Founding editor of Australia's two longest running cricket magazines, *Australian Cricket* (when he was a teenager, in 1968) and *Cricketer* (1973).

John Benaud Richie's younger brother was sacked as NSW captain for continuing to wear a banned set of lightweight ripple-soled adidas cricket shoes, in January 1970. Retired from representative ranks at 29 and became one of Sydney's finest newspapermen. Was also a Test selector, whose refusal to recall an in-form Dean Jones remains a talking point.

Lou Benaud Took 20 wickets in a match, Waratah vs St Mary's, Penrith Showgrounds, Parramatta District Cricket Association, 1923–24. Like his eldest son Richie, Lou bowled leggies.

Richie Benaud Felt so imperilled by the power and ferocity of the cut shots from the likes of the famed 'three Ws' – Everton Weekes, Frank Worrell and Clyde Walcott – that he called for a box while fielding in the gully at Queen's Park Oval, Port of Spain, Trinidad, 1955. *See* Ivan James

Murray Bennett The first Australian cricketer to wear thick-rimmed tinted glasses on the field; the result of eye complications after he'd accidentally rubbed insect repellent into them.

Michael Bevan Made a record eight hundreds with Tasmania in 2004–05, a season in which he aggregated 1464 runs at an average of almost 100.

Andy Bichel Was Australia's 12th man on a record 19 occasions.

Don Bichel Once took a 'seven-for' in a bush international against the touring South Africans at Ipswich, Queensland. His victims included Graeme Pollock, Denis Lindsay and Buster Farrer. Was also wonderfully athletic and reliable in the field and such a sure catch that his mates christened him Spud Hands. At Ipswich one '60s Saturday, opening bowler John Verrankamp had nine wickets, only for Bichel to drop the tenth.

Big Bertha Run-making colossus Bill Ponsford's favourite bat. So 'flattened' was the hitting area, it was once measured to be too wide.

Biscuit man Percy Arnott, the grandson of the founder of the Arnott's Biscuits Company, represented NSW and toured the USA with Arthur Mailey's Australians in autumn 1913, batting in the top six alongside some of

BEST PLAYERS BY THE ALPHABET

A	*Warwick Armstrong*	*M*	*Glenn McGrath*
B	*Don Bradman*	*N*	*Monty Noble*
C	*Greg Chappell*	*O*	*Bill O'Reilly*
D	*Alan Davidson*	*P*	*Ricky Ponting*
E	*Ross Edwards*	*Q*	*Bob Quiney*
F	*Damien Fleming*	*R*	*Ian Redpath*
G	*Adam Gilchrist*	*S*	*Steven Smith*
H	*Neil Harvey*	*T*	*Victor Trumper*
I	*Bert Ironmonger*	*V*	*Adam Voges*
J	*Mitchell Johnson*	*W*	*Shane Warne*
K	*Usman Khawaja*	*Y*	*Graham Yallop*
L	*Dennis Lillee*	*Z*	*Tim Zoehrer*

the game's finest, including Collins, Macartney, Bardsley and the Englishman JN Crawford. Arnott was also a long-time director of his family's empire.

Bob Bitmead The only 'wrong foot' bowler to represent Australia. He delivered his slow left-arm in-swingers and orthodox finger spinners from around the wicket, from wide out on the outside crease. His one international came against New Zealand in an unofficial test in Dunedin in 1967.

Bill Black Conceded 62 runs from two overs on the town's new malthoid wicket as Don Bradman powered to the fastest century of his life, in 18 minutes, for a Blackheath XI vs a Lithgow Pottery XII, Blackheath, NSW, November 1931. Several of young Don's sixes soared over the mature stand of Monterey pines wide of long-on.

Jack Blackham Highly-strung and nervy, Australia's finest early wicketkeeper and occasional captain hated close finishes and often refused to watch the play, instead pacing up and down the dressing room floor like a caged lion. Stood up over the stumps to even the fastest of bowlers, without a long stop. Was hero-worshipped everywhere he played.

Don Blackie An Australian Test player into his mid-forties, he had trouble remembering names, so called everyone 'Rock'.

Scott 'Barrel' Boland At 18, he was a massive 118 kilograms (18½ stone) and was told he'd be a permanent Second XI player at Frankston unless he lost a truckload of weight. He did, and many stepping stones later he took a fairytale six for seven on his Ashes debut in Melbourne, 2021.

Usain Bolt Asked who his all-time sporting hero was, the fastest man in the universe replied: 'Matthew Hayden'.

Sir Henry Bolte Captain of his school's football and cricket teams in Ballarat, he was a member of the Western Plains team which finished runners-up at Ballarat Country Week in 1930. Played cricket into his

47th year, but is better known as being Victoria's longest serving state premier, from 1955–72.

George Bonnor Known as The Colonial Hercules, no one rivalled his ability to smite the ball hard and high into orbit. The biggest hitter of almost any era, he stood 198 centimetres (six foot six) in his socks and towered over most of his contemporaries, but not his two older brothers. They called him Tiny.

Once hit a ball so high in a Test match (1880), he was caught having turned for a third run. An eyewitness said the ball 'dropped like a meteorite from above'. Was said to have once thrown a cricket ball 120 yards (110 metres), while standing in a barrel.

David Boon Drank a record 52 full-strength cans of beer on the flight to Heathrow in 1989 and averaged 55 in the Tests.

Brian Booth A devout Christian, the two-time Australian captain refused to play on Sundays. Also represented Australia at hockey.

Allan Border *See* Captain Grumpy

Dene Border Allan Border's 12-year-old son was playing for Brisbane Boys College against Brisbane State High in the early '90s. Barney Dell, the son of another former Aussie Test player, was also in the team. Having taken guard, young Dene played at and missed his first two deliveries.

'Hey Border,' said the opposition's wicketkeeper, 'you're not as good as your fuckin' old man.'

Francis Bourke The five-time Richmond (VFL) premiership player was in yet another Grand Final, this time for his beloved Canterbury Cricket Club, when, in taking a quick single, he collided with the bowler. Dusting himself off, having safely made his ground, he said to the kid, 'It's not everyone who can say they've been run through by Francis Bourke on Grand Final day.'

Geoff Boycott The famed Yorkshireman made a record seven First XI centuries for Waverley in Sydney grade ranks in 1976–77.

Geoff Boyd Having taken four hat-tricks in seven matches for Pomborneit (near Camperdown, Victoria) in 1939, he received a letter of congratulations from Don Bradman. One of his hat-tricks was a double. In all he took six, his last aged 43. Boyd's career record of 10,000 runs and 1000 wickets is among the very best in the bush. He attended Ballarat Country Week for 33 consecutive years and Melbourne Country Week for 22.

Harry Boyle Representing Eighteen of Victoria, he became the first Australian to clean bowl WG Grace, with a ball which cut back from the leg and struck the doctor's middle stump: Melbourne, December 1873.

Boyley's silly mid-on A revolutionary fielding position invented by Boyle.

Craig Bradley Silky, multiskilled sportsman, among the finest to play both Aussie Rules and cricket at representative levels. He had an agreement with Carlton Football Club in the 1980s that autumn-time club cricket finals would always take precedence over any early season VFL fixtures. Represented Australia Under 19s alongside future Test trio Craig McDermott, Tony Dodemaide and Mike Veletta.

Don Bradman The most iconic batsman of all, scorer of an Australian record 212 centuries at all levels: 29 in Tests, 88 in other first-class matches and 95 in minor games. His first 100, aged 12, came for Bowral High in 1920 and his last, aged 40, for LR Vollugi's XI at St Peter's College in Adelaide in 1948.

His Test average of 99.94 was adopted as the ABC's Australia-wide post office box number.

Had all the chances he offered in Tests been taken, his average would still have been 74.49.

His nicknames included The Don, Braddles, George, Goldie, The Knight, The Boy from Bowral, The Boss, The Great Man, The Wizard of the Willow and, in America, 'the Babe Ruth of cricket'. In 1932–33, Douglas Jardine often referred to him as The Little Bastard.

Dermott Brereton Having seen me turn a comfortable three into a hard-run two, the old footy champ and my friend of 40 years interrupted play and said, 'With all respect Ken, fellas … throw to Piessey's end!' Heatherhill vs Mt Eliza, Emil Madsen Reserve, Mt Eliza, Mornington Peninsula, February 2022.

'Bring Back Deano' A banner bearing this motto continued to be displayed at the Melbourne Cricket Ground for years after the retirement of favourite son Dean Jones.

Tom Brooks Once told Dennis Lillee to 'get back here and bat' after Lillee had summarily decided it was too wet to continue and started walking towards the rooms, without reference to either Brooks or his fellow umpire, first-gamer Dick French: Western Australia vs NSW, Sydney, February 1976.

Bill Brown His one-off stint as captain of Australia lasted barely eight hours on a wet Basin Reserve, NZ, wicket that saw 28 wickets tumble in four sessions in Wellington, 1946. And at the time he didn't even know that it was an official Test. (It wasn't until 1948 that the game was accorded Test status.)

Stan Brown Made five centuries in a row: Yalca North, Nathalia, Victoria, 1937.

William Brown Took 15 wickets in his only first-class match: Tasmania vs Victoria, Lower Domain Ground (Government Paddock), Hobart, March 1858.

Eric Brumby Slept on the side of the wicket on the eve of the North Coast vs New South Wales fixture at Fisher Park to ensure that the sacred turf remain untouched, leading into Grafton's much-awaited spring-time challenge, in October 1951.

Jack Brunton Conceded 49 byes, most of them off Test tearaway Ernie Jones in a South Adelaide First XI club match in 1896–97.

Neil Bulger Amassed 1013 runs at an average of 202 in the Tumut Association (NSW) in 1977–78.

Haydn Bunton Best known as the finest Aussie Rules footballer of the '30s – and one of the game's enduring celebrities – Bunton was also a capital all-round cricketer who was once asked by Bill Ponsford to join his club, St Kilda. In a mid-week fixture at Hurstville Oval in the spring of 1927, a 16-year-old Bunton scored 98 in a match which also featured Don Bradman.

Commenting that night on radio, former Test captain MA (Monty) Noble said, 'The game had two potential Australian Test batsmen in Donald Bradman from Bowral who scored 125 unbeaten and Haydn Bunton from Albury who was stumped making the hit he needed for a much-deserved century.' Named 12 months later for a Southern Riverina XI against the 1928–29 Englishmen at Goulburn, Bunton made five, opening the batting against Harold Larwood.

His record of three Brownlow and three Sandover Medals, two of football's highest awards, is unsurpassed.

Peter Burge Made seven centuries as a 13-year-old schoolboy in Brisbane in 1945–46. A late bloomer, he was dropped from the Australian team six times before he'd played even a dozen Tests.

Arthur Burgess Hit the longest six ever seen in Cobar (in the NSW central west). The ball finished half a mile away and it took a fella on a motor bike 10 minutes to go and fetch it. (So flat and hard was the clay pan around Kerrigundi's cricket ground that having cleared the fence and aided by the wind, the ball bounded away like an old-fashioned superball).

Jim Burke A noted stonewaller, he once blocked for almost six hours for just 48 runs in the first Ashes Test in Brisbane, 1958, dubbed later by Jack Fingleton as The Battle of the Snooze. On another occasion, in Sydney, he was told by a barracker, 'I wish I was a pigeon, Burke, and you were a statue.'

Away from the game, he loved nothing better than playing boogie-woogie piano at parties.

Kenny Burn Named Australia's second wicketkeeper on the 1890 tour of England, despite not having kept wickets in his life. He remains the only Australian club cricketer to score back-to-back triple centuries.

Matthew Burns In his maiden summer, representing the Emu Plains Under 9s (1981–82), eight-year-old Matthew's season analysis was 124–85–69–42. His average was 1.64.

Bushfire test Was held over four days in Melbourne in April, 1967, between the two Australian touring teams which had been to South Africa and New Zealand. More than $30,000 was raised for the Tasmanian Bushfire Relief Fund.

BRISBANE HAPPENINGS

DECEMBER 1993

Ian Healy becomes the first to be given out, run out, via video replay.

DECEMBER 1984

Australia's captain Kim Hughes resigns in tears after Australia is beaten by the world champion West Indian team in four days. A victim of barbs from within and outside the team, he'd won just four of his 28 Tests in charge.

NOVEMBER 1974

Clem Jones, the Lord Mayor of Brisbane, sacks the curator and prepares the Test wicket himself, leading into the eventful opening Test of the 1974–75 Ashes summer, in which Australia unleashed for the first time its most lethal new-ball pairing of Dennis Lillee and Jeff Thomson.

DECEMBER 1963

Mysteriously recalled after years outside the Test team, Ian Meckiff is no-balled for throwing on multiple occasions in his only over and retires immediately. Meckiff admits years later that he was set up, at a time when many Test teams were fielding bowlers with doubtful actions.

MID-YEAR 1931

International and interstate matches are moved away from the Brisbane Exhibition Ground to the Gabba, in part because of a lost revenue stream after members of the Royal National Association gained free admission to the city's earliest Test matches.

Caffyn to Cullinan

Billy Caffyn Surrey-born, he was Australia's most notable early international coach who remained in Melbourne in 1864 after the second of his two tours Down Under with the earliest English XIs. Among the rising youngsters he mentored was Test cricket's first centurion, Charles Bannerman.

Bill Cahill Ambidextrous, he bowled both right and left hand slows against the touring South Africans in the same over during his only Tasmanian 'international' at the NTCA ground in Launceston, January 1932.

Norman Callaway Scored a record 207 in his only first-class innings with New South Wales in February 1915 and soon afterwards was killed in action during World War I. Originally from Hay, close to the Murrumbidgee River in the western Riverina, a double of 117 and 64 for the local public school prompted one local newspaper writer to call him 'the Trumper of the school'. He was just 14 years old.

Blair Campbell Was noted on the hottest, high summer days at Prahran's Toorak Park of 'disappearing' from his boundary-riding duties at deep third man into the home rooms for a quick cold shower before re-emerging to bowl the next over, dripping wet. Represented two states and was also a prominent Aussie Rules forward, noted for his ability to kick boomerang goals from the boundary line.

Captain Grumpy Allan Border. Teammate Andrew Symonds liked to call him Grandpa Smurf.

Alex Carey Australia's present Test wicketkeeper, he debuted with Glenelg's First XI, aged 15, in 1996.

Has made centuries in six different grades at Glenelg: Under 13s, Under 14s, Under 17s and A, B and D grades. A Glenelg Reserves Premiership footballer, he was also part of Greater Western Sydney's senior AFL training squad before being released.

Keith Carmody Inventor of the 'Carmody' or the 'umbrella' field, the Australian Services batsman and first Sheffield Shield–winning Western Australian captain spent two days in a rubber dinghy in the Atlantic before becoming a prisoner of war, having been shot down during World War II.

Sammy Carter As durable a wicketkeeper as Australia has ever had and the first to squat on his haunches to ease the strain on his legs, one of his fitness rituals was his daily swim at Bondi Beach, summer and winter. Was 54 when he kept wickets on Arthur Mailey's American tour in 1932. Worked as an undertaker.

Alvisio Casagrande Made a comeback on the hard wickets of the Mornington Peninsula, Victoria, with an artificial forearm joint clicking into his elbow, allowing him to again hold a bat. Having fallen asleep at the wheel and ploughed into a tree, he'd broken his leg and so badly injured his lower right arm that it had to be amputated. 'Suddenly I was playing straighter as I had to grip the bat handle harder with my left hand,' he said. A post-accident high of 90 with Main Ridge's Second XI was celebrated like a double century.

Caught Marsh, bowled Lillee Their record of 95 Test dismissals is unequalled. Ian Chappell rates Rod Marsh and Dennis Lillee among Australia's all-time finest. 'They were talented, aggressive and determined and weren't prepared to bow to any opposition,' he said. 'They gave their all for both country and state. Great characters, great cricketers.'

Craig Chambers Mentone Grammar's scorer when it won the Melbourne Associated Grammar Schools First XI premiership in 1986–87. The ultimate cricket aficionado, Craig suffers from cerebral palsy and it could take him upwards of 15 minutes to walk across the ground from the scorer's box to the luncheon room at Keysborough, south of Melbourne. Shane Warne was the school's cricket captain and star bowler. He would always drive around to the box to pick Craig up so he could have lunch with the players. 'He was a mate's mate,' said Craig. 'If you were in his circle, you knew it. He appreciated everyone who was on the journey with him.'

Garry Chapman Scored 17 all run, without any overthrows, after a ball was lost in 25 centimetre (10 inch) long grass: Banyule vs Macleod, Heidelberg C, fifth grade, Winsor Reserve, October 1990. 'No-one yelled "lost ball" so we just ran six, then another six and walked five more for the heck of it,' said Chapman. It took him just six scoring shots to make 28.

Greg Chappell The first Australian to 7000 Test runs. His nine-slip cordon for New Zealand tailender Peter Petherick in an Auckland Test was stage-managed to add an extra illustration for his 1977 book *The 100th Summer*. Reserve paceman Alan Hurst took the picture.

Trevor Chappell Asked once which of his brothers was the better captain, Trevor commented, 'Ian never asked me to bowl underarm.'

Jack Charlton Batting at Fish Creek one day, he drilled one into the outfield and dashed up and down the wicket five times. His partner, George Savage, wasn't as agile and had completed only three when the ball was finally retrieved. Doomburrim vs Tarwin, South Gippsland, 1955–56.

Jack Chegwyn Led 150 cricket tours to country NSW and beyond from 1939 into the 1960s, playing celebrity games and assisting in unearthing the next generations of NSW bush champions. Matches were played on all sorts of surfaces, even one on an airport tarmac, at Iron Range on the Cape York Peninsula.

Ben Chifley Australia's prime minister subsidised the rent for new British arrival Harold Larwood, his wife and five daughters in 1950. The old Bodyliner was surprised that his initial rent was just 16 pounds and didn't learn of Chifley's generosity until many years later.

Hugh Chilvers Played with Northern District's First XI into his 57th year, amassing 1153 wickets and taking 105 'five-for's. Both feats are Sydney first-grade records. Took 100 wickets or more in three consecutive seasons early in World War II, including 126 in 1942–43 when one-day games were scheduled. Averaged four wickets per game at first-class level, but tended to play mainly when Bill O'Reilly was away or unavailable. Was an unlucky omission from Australia's 1930 Ashes tour and was stopped from touring India with Frank Tarrant's Australians in 1935–36 by a short-sighted, bombastic administration.

Don Chipp The pride of Northcote High and prominent parliamentarian, Chipp loved cricket and was a regular in the Prime Minister's XI matches in the '50s and early '60s, including in Don Bradman's final game in February 1963. He dined out on the fact that he batted at number four that day, with the Don at number five!

Arthur Chipperfield A dashing batsman, unstoppable at his best, he became the first Australian debutant to be dismissed for 99 in an Ashes Test at Trent Bridge in 1934. Undefeated on 99 at lunch, he was caught behind third ball after the interval from the bowling of the 196 cm (six foot five) Ken Farnes without adding to his score. He'd missed a loose legside delivery from Farnes the ball before.

Dan Christian Has played for a record 16 Twenty20 franchises worldwide – at last count.

Peter Civitella Won the Williamstown and District's A grade bowling trophy in 2003–04 with 30 economical wickets, despite having only one full arm, his left.

Belinda Clark The first to hit a double century in an ODI: World Cup, Australia vs Denmark, Middle Income Group Ground, Mumbai, December 1997.

Tony Clark Even an artificial leg didn't stop him from being a regular Saturday afternoon club cricketer in the Huon competition, just outside Hobart, in the '70s. Opposing teams allowed him to bat with a runner.

Michael Clarke So promising was the Western Suburbs and NSW teen that he was signed to a long-term near million-dollar bat contract with Slazenger before he'd played even one Test.

Billy Coghlan The first known 75-year-old to take a triple hat-trick: five wickets with five balls at Bulleen, Melbourne, 1999–2000.

Arthur Coningham Claimed a wicket with his first ball in his only Test in Melbourne, December 1894.

Learie Constantine On the rest day of the fifth Test in Sydney, in March 1931, Constantine and West Indian teammate Clifford Roach ventured to Jervis Bay for an impromptu cricket match organised by local Huskisson hotelier Frank O'Brien and the ex-Australian international Arthur Mailey. While rain forced a considerable early delay, Constantine entertained by juggling and showing how to take a catch behind his back. He also gave a skipping demonstration. According to *The Shoalhaven Telegraph*, almost everyone had an autograph book and the visiting stars were kept busy signing their names. One member of the local XI was the Ginger Meggs creator, James Bancks. His sketches of 'Ginge' could be seen alongside the names of the Test players.

John Conway As a teenager he bowled the first ball in the very first colonial 'international' for XVIII of Victoria against England in Melbourne in 1861. One of the early giants of the colonial game and sole selector of the Combined Australian team which contested the first Ashes Test, he was also the highly successful entrepreneur and manager of the 1880 tour to England and beyond which stretched for 13 months and grossed each player up to 1000 guineas – the equivalent at the time to five years of 'Monday to Friday' wages. Wrote for *The Australasian* under the pseudonym Censor. Was prickly, pugnacious and polarising. Only seven attended his funeral in out-of-the-way Frankston, Victoria.

Claude Corbett High-profile between-the-wars cricket writer for the Sydney *Sun*, responsible for the biggest 'scoop' story of all at the height of the Bodyline furore when Australia's cricket captain Bill Woodfull told England's mighty man of Empire, the soon-to-be-knighted PF 'Plum' Warner in Adelaide that 'there were two teams out there, and only one is playing cricket'.

Sam Cosstick His bowling analysis of 21.1–20–1–6 in a Victoria vs Tasmania match in Melbourne, 1869, is the most extraordinary of all. A professional bowler with the Melbourne CC, he did not concede a run until his twentieth over. The all-amateur Tasmanian XI was all out for 18. (Overs then consisted of four balls.)

Jack Cottam The youngest, at 19, of Australia's 72 'one-Test wonders'. Had played only one major match before his shock call-up in Sydney, February 1887.

Tibby Cotter The fast sling bowler had a habit of breaking stumps and the fingers of opposing batsmen. In one club match, North Sydney's Stud White was hospitalised after taking a Cotter thunderbolt squarely on his top hand. 'Well, that's one of the bastards out of the way,' said Cotter. Much to his surprise, White returned an hour later. 'Give me that ball,' said Cotter. 'I'll break the bastard's neck this time.'

George Coulthard Umpired a Test match (1879), before playing in one (1882). Another all-round sportsman, Paddy McShane, was also to achieve the same feat soon afterwards.

Ed Cowan Made a double century as a 14-year-old for Cranbrook school, Sydney, in the mid-'90s on his way to Sheffield Shield and Test honours.

Bob Cowper Relegated to 12th man late in the 1965–66 Ashes series – he'd been told by Australia's selection chairman Sir Donald Bradman he was unfit – Cowper responded in the very next Test with an MCG-record 307 including 27 threes. Known as 'Wallaby', after his father who played rugby union for Australia, Cowper took part in the world real tennis tournament at Hayling Island, Hampshire, in 1984. For many years he lived in Monaco.

Ian Craig Asked by Don Bradman to lead Australia's touring team to South Africa in 1957–58, Craig's appointment, at 22, almost caused a mutiny among his playing elders. 'You don't say no to Don Bradman,'

Craig told me. As a 17-year-old he'd become the youngest Australian to make a first-class double century, against the touring 1952–53 South Africans. Remains Australia's youngest debutant and captain. Wore size 7 shoes. Was born in Yass, near Canberra.

The Cricketers Arms One of Richmond's most famed hotels, it is situated directly opposite the Melbourne Cricket Ground.

Alexander Crooks Became the hero of all Adelaide after catching cricket's champion WG Grace on the ropes at the Adelaide Oval in 1874. Bathing in his new exalted social status, he was soon managing the Commercial Bank of South Australia, only for it go into liquidation and Crooks to jail for misappropriating funds and lending money to too many mates.

Crown Street Superior Public School The Sydney school nestling just north-west of the SCG was attended by a young Victor Trumper. His first recorded match for the school was as an 11-year-old in 1888.

Don Cullinan Made the best 38 of his life against the touring West Indies in Mildura in 1981–82 after telling Michael Holding to 'stop bowling half pace' and let them go like he was in a Test match. He wanted to truly test himself against the fastest bowler in the world.

Darling to Dyson

Joe Darling He was one day short of his 15th birthday when he scored 252 for Prince Alfred College against St Peter's at the Adelaide Oval in 1885. Later captained Australia. Was the first Test skipper to make a pair (Sheffield, 1902) and the first Australian to be immortalised in wax at Madame Tussauds. Campaigned successfully to have hits over the fence awarded as 'six'. Kept himself fit in retirement in Hobart chopping firewood into his seventies. Possessed a set of *Wisden*.

Rick Darling Struck under the heart by a Bob Willis bouncer in Adelaide, 1979, he collapsed and almost choked when his chewing gum lodged in his throat. Only quick action from umpire Max O'Connell and one of the English fielders, John Emburey, averted a calamity.

Alan Davidson The first Australian to take a 'ten-for' and make a hundred in representative cricket: Australia B vs Wairarapa CA, Masterton, NZ, 1949–50.

Geoff Davies Close but no cigar: one of an elite group of Aussie 12th men (Brisbane, 1968) not to play a Test.

Ian Davis Nowra's 'boy wonder', he made his first century at 10, captained NSW and Australia Under 14s, took a 'ten-for' and, in 1967–68, aged 14, broke the rare 1000-runs-in-a-season barrier with 1066 runs at 266 for Trojan Blacks in the Shoalhaven Under 15s competition. Six years later he was awarded a NSW and a Test cap in his maiden season of first-class cricket. Only four others had also played Tests during their first representative year. Nicknamed The Wizard.

Ken Davis A pillar of University's middle order in Melbourne in the 1970s, he made a pair as the normally strong Uni team was beaten outright by St Kilda early on the second day at the Junction Oval. In brilliant early-summer sunshine, it was agreed to play a 20-overs practice game, Davis only just avoiding scoring three ducks in the same game when an outside edge whistled through a vacant third slip area.

Clem Davison Broken Hill's Mr Cricket, he made 307 not out for St Peters vs Returned Soldiers, in November 1919. It remains a record for Silver City cricket.

John Davison A Canadian-born spinning allrounder for two Sheffield Shield states, his 67-ball century for Canada against the West Indies at Centurion in the 2003 World Cup was toasted around the world.

Deafy Don Tallon's nickname. During the 1953 Coronation Year tour, captain Lindsay Hassett sent him out in poor light with the instructions to 'give the light a go'. He tried to belt everything over the grandstand and was soon out. When queried, he told Hassett, 'I thought you wanted me to have a go.'

Travis Dean Started his Sheffield Shield career in spectacular fashion, making 154 not out and 109 not out while opening for Victoria against Queensland in Melbourne, 2015.

Tony Dell The first Test cricketer to have seen active service in Vietnam, Dell was born in the UK on 6 August, 1945, the day Hiroshima was bombed.

Christened Anthony Ross Hiroshima Dell, he ditched the 'Hiroshima' during his high-school days in Brisbane. 'I didn't like it,' he said.

Later, when trialling for Queensland's Shield team, he put his birthdate 'forward' by two years, having been told that a younger player would attract more interest.

The Demon Fred Spofforth.

Michael Di Venuto Represented Australia and Italy.

Billy Dick One of Melbourne's finest Federation-era sportsmen, he made five First XI hundreds for Carlton CC in District cricket ranks, despite being blind in one eye.

Walter Dight The oldest Sydney first-grade player to take a 'five-for'. He was 52 when he took five for 68 representing Western Suburbs against Central Cumberland in 1922–23.

Xavier Doherty First played A grade cricket at 12, for George Town on the Tamar in north-east Tasmania.

Doing a 'Bo Derek' (a perfect 10; 10 for 0): LG (Bo) Allen, Bittern vs Somerville, Bittern, Victoria, 1946–47; J Burr, Strathmore Under 12s vs Strathmore North, Victoria, 1962–63; R Morgan, Beachport Colts vs Cellulose CC, Millicent, SA, 1968–69; and Errol Hall, Australian Hotels vs Tannymorel, Warwick, Queensland, 1986–87.

Dolly The MCC's horse, responsible for pulling the giant roller in the '20s and '30s. Every time she saw Bert

Ironmonger come out to bat at number 11, she'd start to get restless. Rarely would old Bert last even one over. His career average was 2.62.

Harry Donnan The old Australian Ashes tourist amassed the highest score ever by a 43-year-old with 353 for Bexley Oriental against Bexley: St George CA, December 1908.

Bruce Dooland Adelaide-born and bred, he taught Richie Benaud the flipper. Took 100-plus wickets in five consecutive seasons of English county cricket with Nottinghamshire in the 1950s.

Brett Dorey His colourful European CV before his maiden matches for Western Australia at 28 and Australia at 29 included being bodyguard to the children of a wealthy Russian businessman. Imposingly built at 203 centimetres (six foot eight), he was impossible to miss in any crowd.

Gordon Dorrough Scored 3000-plus runs at an average of 72 with 14 centuries in four seasons for Thornleigh, near Hornsby in Sydney, in the late 1950s.

Bryan Doyle The first shearer chosen to play for Victoria, for six matches in 1994–95.

John Drennan Among those chosen to tour with the Australia team without playing a Test. A fast bowler from Adelaide, he was a back-up in Ian Craig's 1957–58 team to tour South Africa but appeared in only half the games.

Wally Dudley Dismissed Don Bradman first ball in only his second interstate match on Christmas Day, 1940.

Reg Duff The only Australian to make a Test century from number 10: Melbourne, 1902. It was his debut Test.

Ross Duncan Noted for bowling in silky women's bloomers, he broke down on the eve of his only official Test match, but played anyway and limped through just 14 overs without taking a wicket, in Melbourne, January 1971.

John Dyson His stunning outfield catch to dismiss West Indian Sylvester Clarke remains among the finest ever witnessed at the Sydney Cricket Ground. Leaping like a soccer goalie, Dyson hung in the air as the ball soared over his head and falling backwards, clutched it with both hands in front of the old Sydney 'Hill'. 'It's one of the best outfield catches you'll ever see,' said Bill Lawry on *Channel 9*, January 1982.

HARRY DONNAN'S RECORD SCORE

BEXLEY ORIENTAL vs BEXLEY

St George Cricket Association A grade | *5 & 12 December 1908*

BEXLEY ORIENTAL

H Veale	c Birch, b Rose	0	W Kenwood	run out	71
A Cooper	c Lardner, b Smith	228	B Wright	b Rose	0
H Scope	b Rose	3	J McGarry	not out	24
A Thompson	b Rose	0	J Farr	not out	5
H Donnan	c & b Rose	353	Sundries		23
A Harrison	b Birch	42	Total		9–784

Fall: 2, 16, 16, 422, 537, 600, 745, 745, 771

BOWLING: W Rose 39-4-168-5, T Brierley 23-1-106-0, A Smith 29-3-180-1, S Tuckwell 8-0-63-0, O Dadswell 18-0-107-0, A Birch 7-1-27-1, A Preddy 7-1-41-1, C Lardner 2-0-25-0 (the bowling analysis is 44 runs short)

Did not bowl: H Cox, AN Other, C Rogers

Stumps Day 1: Bexley Oriental 3–241. They then batted through the entire second day.

Scoreboard: Alf James

Eady to Exelby

Charles Eady The Champion of the South, his 566 for Break O'Day against Wellington CC remains the highest solo score in senior Australian club cricket. He hit 13 fives, 68 fours and was dropped six times, the match going into an unscheduled fourth Saturday to allow two full innings to be completed, at Hobart Domain, autumn 1902.

Barry Eastment A prominent first-grader at Gordon, Sydney, he took eight wickets on a matting wicket at Harvard University against the touring Pakistani team, which had been in the West Indies for a Test series in 1957–58. Was also selected for the USA for its annual 'test' match with Canada.

Ken Eastwood First selected at 35, he hitchhiked to his only Test match when the team taxis failed to arrive. While he failed in both innings, he did take an important wicket with his left-arm chinamans in Sydney 1971. Years earlier he'd taken four wickets in four balls at Melbourne subdistrict First XI level for Williamstown vs Ormond, 1963–64. Originally from Sydney, as a 16-year-old at Gordon he once made 320 and took eight for 38 in a schoolboy's match.

Jack Edwards A stonewaller, selected directly from Bendigo club cricket, he made a record 15 ducks during the 1888 Ashes tour.

Wally Edwards The first Australian Test cricketer since the Don to serve as Cricket Australia's chairman.

Eight all run Cec Starr and Roy Lonergan: Adelaide vs East Torrens, Adelaide Oval, late '30s.

An Eight-Saturday Grand Final Asquith 407 & 332 lost to Thornleigh 278 & 470, by nine runs: Hornsby, Ku-ring-gai and Hills District B grade, 1952–53.

Eighteen-minute hundreds Laurie Quinlan, Cairns, 1909–10; and Russell Penny, for the Malcheks XI against the Garbutt Magpies at the Goldfield Ashes, Charters Towers, 1986. Penny's hundred came from 23 balls. He scored 133 overall; all but five runs coming in boundaries. Shoalhaven's Neil Watt registered a 19-minute century in the immediate post-war years at Albion Park, NSW.

Eighteen runs off one ball Old-time bush grounds, especially paddocks, often had a tree or two in play. At Coraki, NSW, one day in the 1870s, a ball lodged in a parrot's nest high up in a cleft of a gum. The batsmen started to run up and down the wicket. Suddenly a fielder called, 'Lost ball!' which would have limited the runs to six.

'No,' said the umpire. 'We can all see it.'

The batsmen continued to run and finally one of the fielders scaled the tree, retrieved the ball and threw it to a fielder, who appealed.

'Howzaaat?'

'Out,' said the umpire, but not before 18 runs had been recorded.

Henry Ellem Known as Mr Cricket of the Northern Rivers region of NSW. Took 3000 wickets with his left-arm finger spinners in and around Grafton. Was 'Underwood-like' on the ant-bed wickets of the southern tableland. Co-piloted the Ellem family XI's post-war Christmas week fixtures all over country Queensland. *See* Umpiring pearlers

Craig Elliot Geelong City CC's long-time '90s president insisted on players wearing correct club apparel. He would sell jumpers, caps and shirts over the boundary fence to fielders even during a game. The fielder would try on several sizes between overs, then be handed the correct fit ... and an account! Invariably the club made a profit.

Gideon Elliott His nine for two remains among the most extraordinary figures in the first 175 years of Australian first-class cricket: Victoria vs Tasmania, Launceston, February 1858.

Jack Ellis An Ashes tourist in 1926 without playing a Test, he worked in Melbourne as a building contractor and often used Friday mornings to quote on inner-city jobs once he knew that Victoria was batting first. With a formidable top four of Woodfull, Ponsford, Hendry and Ryder, never once was he caught out. When Victoria amassed a world record 1107 against NSW in 1927–28, his pull shot to deep midwicket brought up the 1000.

'That's three for me and 1000 for Victoria,' he said. 'Long live Victoria.'

Herb Elphinston Mistakenly gave NSW's Billy Watson not out after he tickled his second ball behind to Godfrey Evans, standing over the stumps to Alec Bedser. Watson, 23 years old, made 155 and within weeks was selected for Australia in 1954–55. 'It was a big game,' Watson said years later, 'and a second ball duck wouldn't have looked quite as good.'

Phil Emery The first NSW wicketkeeper to 300 career dismissals. Was brave, resilient and skilled. Played a one-off Test for Australia.

William Redvers Evison Known to everyone as Ref, he and his brother Mel took all 20 wickets in a game against Berry, NSW, in 1928–29, and on 11 other occasions the pair accounted for all wickets in an innings, although there was the occasional run out. When he got his hand caught in a chaffcutter on his farm in 1930 it was feared his career was over, but he found a way to grip the bat and hit a club record 234 against Perseverance in 1931–32.

His middle name came from a general in the Boer War, which was being fought in South Africa at the time of his birth in 1900.

Bill Exelby Was curator for 53 years at Queen Elizabeth Oval, Bendigo's pride-and-joy cricket ground and the venue for many 'bush internationals'.

EXPERTS

Expert first slipsmen

Hugh Trumble, Jack Gregory, Bobby Simpson, Ian Chappell, Mark Taylor. (Gregory took 13 catches against England in the 1920–21 Ashes series.)

...

Expert second slipsmen

Keith Miller, Greg Chappell, Allan Border, Mark Waugh, Ricky Ponting, Steve Smith.

...

Expert gully fieldsmen

Ian Redpath, Ashley Mallett, Geoff Marsh, Richie Benaud, Matthew Hayden, Mike Hussey.

...

Expert nightwatchmen

Jason Gillespie, Nathan Lyon, Tony Mann, Kerry O'Keeffe, Hugh Trumble.

...

Expert tossers

MA (Monty) Noble, Lindsay Hassett, Mark Taylor. (They won all five tosses in a five-Test series.)

...

Expert commentators

Alan McGilvray, Richie Benaud, Ian Chappell, Melanie Jones, Jim Maxwell.

...

Expert 12th men

Andy Bichel, Ray Bright, Michael Neser, Brad Hodge.

Fahey to Fury

Geoff Fahey The Crookwell farmer averaged five hundreds a year for 18 seasons and played three matches against overseas touring teams.

Family XIs Bassett (Arthurs Creek, Victoria), Bidgood (Miles, Queensland), Bight (Mirboo, Gippsland), Ellem (Upper Macleay, Northern Rivers, NSW), Hodgetts (West Ridgley, Burnie, Tasmania), Jeffrey (Goulburn, NSW), Lang (Warrion, Victoria), Lawrie (Gresford, Maitland, NSW), McConchie (Richmond, Victoria), Mobbs (Carlingford, Sydney), Richardson (Sandford, Tasmania), Thompson (French Island, Western Port Bay, Victoria) and Veivers (Toowoomba, Queensland).

Fastest into-the-wind bowler of all time On a whim, Australia's captain Ian Chappell threw the ball to Jeff Thomson to bowl into the wind at the Gabba in the first Test of 1974–75. He'd always intended to use Dennis Lillee downwind from the Stanley Street end, coupled with Max (Tangles) Walker from Vulture Street. 'Hang on, Tang … you have a go, Thommo,' he said, the athletic Queenslander bowling at intimidating high speeds throughout to take nine match-winning wickets in his memorable maiden Ashes Test.

Les Favell Frustrated at the lack of representative opportunities in hometown Sydney, he moved to Adelaide and, on debut against a star-studded NSW team – from the state that refused to select him – scored 86 and 164 in Adelaide, November 1951. He was soon in the Test team.

Felix The nom de plume used by Tom Horan in his colourful writings for *The Australasian* in the late nineteenth and early twentieth centuries.

Bill Ferguson Scored 204 Tests and toured 43 times home and away as scorer–baggageman. Died at 77, soon after the release of his autobiography *Mr Cricket* in 1957.

Aaron Finch No Australian has captained more Twenty20 internationals.

Jack Fingleton Controversially omitted from the 1934 Ashes tour – a decision he blamed on Don Bradman – he became the first Australian to score centuries in four consecutive Tests, in 1935 and 1936. Later wrote *Cricket Crisis* (1946), acclaimed as the finest post-war Australian cricket book.

Five hundred and twenty-one runs for the first wicket Henry Gunstone (334) and Herbie Bourke (201): St Andrews vs Methodists, Centenary Park, Ararat 1965–66.

Damien Fleming But for a rare Shane Warne fluff at slip, he would have finished with two Test hat-tricks.

Doug Ford Wicketkeeper and the only regular member of the star-studded NSW team of the late '50s and early '60s not to play Tests.

Andy Fox Took 1000-plus career wickets, playing and mentoring well into his octogenarian years for Fox Valley in the Hornsby region of Sydney.

Bruce Francis His impressive playing CV, featuring a double century for Australia, was overshadowed by his masterminding and managing of Kim Hughes's two controversial 'rebel' tours to South Africa in the mid-'80s.

Eric Freeman Within a week of arriving home from the 1968 Ashes tour, Freeman was selected for his football team Port Adelaide and kicked two goals in the second semifinal, coming off the bench.

Fred Freer Once took nine for three in a Lancashire League game, for Rishton. The Carlton allrounder played one Test as a fill-in in 1946–47.

Ted Fulmer The local baker and bread-deliverer in Berowra, he religiously provided local players with bread rolls and hot dogs every Saturday night in the 1930s.

Lloyd Furphy One of South Gippsland's most stylish batsmen, he made twin centuries in the 1949–50 Grand Final, but his team, Dumbalk North, still lost.

Brian Fury The Iverson of Mildura, he once took six for 57 against a travelling Victorian XI in the early '50s.

The G to Gunstone

The G The Melbourne Cricket Ground, home of the Boxing Day Test match for half a century.

The Gabba The Brisbane Cricket Ground, situated in the Brisbane suburb of Woolloongabba.

Peter, John & James Gambrill Identical triplets born in 1934, they all played for Shore school in Sydney in the immediate post-war years.

Mike Gandy A first-class cricketer and a Test match umpire, he was standing in the deciding women's Ashes Test in Bendigo, January 1985, when England's number three, Carole Hodges, having completed a second run, asked if he happened to be carrying a safety pin.

'Yes, I do have one,' said Mike. 'What do you need it for?'

'I've broken my bra strap. Can you fix it?'

'No,' said Mike, realising that he and Carol could easily land on the back page of the next day's Melbourne *Sun News-Pictorial*.

He called over one of the Australians, Denise Emerson, who duly completed the on-field repairs.

Jo Garey Her one-off Test, for Australia against New Zealand in 1996, lasted just eight overs. She didn't bat or bowl. Scheduled for three days at North Melbourne's Arden Street Oval, the match was washed out after less than half an hour.

George Garnsey One of the first and most significant early Australian cricket book collectors, his Golden Age–era library was described as 'unequalled in its rarity'.

G

Tom Garrett At 18, he remains Australia's youngest ever Ashes player.

Harry Gartung Legend has it that one of his express bouncers at Thornleigh Oval touched a batsman's cap and flew over the boundary on the full for six: Hornsby, Ku-ring-gai and Hills District, late 1920s.

Barney Gatenby Was joined, aged 44, by his two sons Peter and David in the Midlands First XI in senior northern Tasmanian grade ranks in 1968–69. Both boys were to advance to first-class cricket.

Ron Gaunt Took a wicket with his first over in a Test, with his ninth ball ... after two earlier no balls, at Kingsmead, Durban, January 1958.

Brett Geeves The colourful Tasmanian was forced into premature retirement before his 30th birthday, declaring his back was 'as stable as the Egyptian government'. His two Australian appearances were both at white-ball level, one in Darwin.

Stephen Gibbs The 'Bradman' of cricket bibliographers, noted for his extraordinary scholarship, accuracy and passion. His Gibbs Index, held in the Melbourne Cricket Club library, runs to 1900 pages.

George Giffen The first to make 10,000 representative runs and take 1000 wickets.

Ashley Gilbert At 209 centimetres (six foot ten), the Victorian fast bowler remains, with NSW's Phil Alley, the tallest Australian to play first-class cricket.

Eddie Gilbert The Indigenous Barambah man took seven for 16 in his headlining maiden Brisbane Country Week appearance in 1930 and within 12 months was playing for Queensland. Generated explosive pace from just half a dozen steps with his whirring, ultra-quick arm action. Once dismissed Don Bradman for a duck. Was just as lethal without boots.

Adam Gilchrist The only Australian to hit 100 sixes in Tests. Only Kiwi-born pair Brendon McCullum (NZ) and Ben Stokes (England) have hit more. Was also the first wicketkeeper to be officially ranked the number one batsman in the world, in 2002.

William Giles The first replacement, or eleventh-hour selection, for Australia on tour: Australians vs Gentlemen of Scotland, the Grange ground, Edinburgh, 1880. He was studying at Edinburgh University at the time and was a member of the University CC. The Australians initially fielded with 10 before Giles's arrival.

Jason Gillespie Australia's ultimate nightwatchman, he made an astonishing double century in his last Test, in Chittagong, 2006. Two years earlier, when reaching a half-century for the first time in his 59th Test, Gillespie celebrated by jubilantly 'riding' his bat down the Gabba wicket, Happy Gilmore style. He is Australia's greatest Indigenous player.

Gary Gilmour Could swing the ball around corners. Once took six for 14 in a World Cup semifinal in Leeds, UK, 1975.

John Gleeson Dubbed The Tamworth Twister, Gleeson was a master of disguise, his array of leg breaks and wrong 'uns being flicked from his bent middle finger, *à la* 1950s mystery bowler Jack Iverson. The sharpest opposing batsmen learned to listen for the 'fizz' – always a characteristic of the Gleeson wrong 'un.

One of the great characters of his time, he walked in to bat at Lord's in 1972 and was asked if he wanted centre.

'No thanks,' said Gleeson, 'I've played here before.'

His captain Ian Chappell christened him 'CHO': Cricket Hours Only. Even on tour, John preferred his own company and was rarely seen after 6 p.m.

Richie Benaud had recommended he trial in Sydney after Gleeson, then 20, impressed for Gunnedah vs Jack Chegwyn's XI in a charity game in 1961. Facing him in the nets for the first time at the SCG, Benaud was bowled first ball by an off break he'd misread as a leggie.

Don Bradman faced him in the nets in Adelaide one day, using an umbrella as a bat, and was so impressed he immediately fast-tracked Gleeson into the Test team.

Malcolm Gorman Scored in 544 matches for Western Suburbs CC in Sydney.

Gorringe's Game Medium-paced Western Australian swing bowler Harry Gorringe experienced his '15 minutes of fame' with a career-best eight for 56 against Queensland at the WACA Ground at Christmas, 1952. Having taken four for 0 at the head of Queensland's second innings, he finished with three wickets in four balls as the visitors, set 244, were bowled out 100 runs short. He took 11 wickets in the match of his life.

Zoe Goss Dismissed world number one Brian Lara in a charity match: Bradman XI vs a World XI, Sydney Cricket Ground, 1994.

The Governor–General Charles Macartney.

Harry Graham The only Australian to score Ashes centuries in his maiden Tests in Australia and England. Dubbed The Little Dasher.

Leigh Gray Struck 41 runs from a six-ball over. It included one no ball: Banksia vs Rosanna, James Reserve, Melbourne 2001–02.

Graydens Road Oval Renamed the RM Hooper Oval in the mid-'80s, it hosted a shock loss by international touring team Sri Lanka to a local Victorian Country XI in 1989. It is the only turf wicket on the Mornington Peninsula.

Terry Green Scored 540 runs without being dismissed in four consecutive matches for Litchfield vs Granite Flat, Donald & District, Victoria early 1970s.

'Carji' Greeves Best known for winning the VFL's inaugural Brownlow Medal in 1924, he was a gifted cricketer who once made 72 for Geelong College against a visiting English team. In the 1925 Melbourne Country Week, he averaged 108 with two centuries, one a double.

Sir Norman Gregg A NSW representative cricketer on the eve of World War I, he discovered the effects of rubella on unborn children.

Charles Gregory From the most notable early cricketing family, Gregory was the first Australian to make 300 runs in a day: NSW vs Queensland, Brisbane, November 1906. Unlike his father Ned, a member of Australia's first Test XI, the closest Gregory came to national selection was as '14th man' on the eve of the fourth Ashes Test in 1901–02.

Jack Gregory The glamour boy of Australian cricket in the 1920s: the fastest bowler, surest catcher and cleanest big-hitter, Gregory preferred not to use batting gloves or a box. A century against South Africa in Johannesburg in 1921 came in just 70 minutes.

Ken Grieves Made 23,099 first-class runs, the most by any Australian without playing a Test.

Clarrie Grimmett The first to 200 Test wickets, the Dunedin-born leg-spinning journeyman bowled more balls per Test – 392 – than any other Australian, ahead of long-time spin partner Bill O'Reilly (371), John Gleeson (305) and Richie Benaud (303). His biographer, Ashley Mallett, titled Grimmett's life story *The Bradman of Spin*.

Tim Grosser Made back-to-back double centuries in bush cricket in the Semi and Grand finals for Gunnedah in north-west NSW, 1962–63.

Tom Groube Chosen for an Ashes touring squad directly out of Melbourne club ranks, 1880.

Nelma Grout The first woman to umpire a senior A grade Brisbane club game, in 1976–77. She was Wally's daughter.

Wally Grout Australia's most loved post-war wicketkeeper, known for often running to fine leg, pads and all, to retrieve snicks and glances. His gambling addiction made him hock all his equipment to meet bookmaker debts from two tours to England. Once he got into a conversation with a well-spoken English gent who was telling him how he'd been educated at Eton and Oxford. 'And what about you, Wal?'

'Eatin' and drinkin',' came the reply.

Colin Guest Once took eight for five in a First XI club match for Melbourne, 1961–62. Played a one-off Test for Australia as a third paceman, 12 months later.

Donald Gumm Representing Bomaderry, NSW, he averaged 100 plus in five consecutive Shoalhaven junior seasons in the '80s. In three of these seasons his average was 200 plus.

Dean Gunawardana Made a century, all in fours and sixes, for Silverton Under 11s, Dandenong District CA, 1997–98.

Henry Gunstone The Ararat legend scored 129 centuries, the majority in northern Victoria. One came on his wedding day. His career best was 334. Once he made four 100s on the first four days of Ballarat Country Week, only to be dismissed for a duck on Day Five, in the Grand Final.

Others at minor level to reach the 100 hundreds milestone include Geoff Fahey, Ray Gartrell, Peter Mattey, Roy Millar, Les Quarrell, Ron Salter, Sam Scuderi and Les Windridge. *See also* Five hundred and twenty-one runs for the first wicket

GROUNDS

Test cricket grounds mentioned in this book.

AUSTRALIA

- Bellerive Oval (Blundstone Arena), Hobart, Tasmania
- Brisbane Exhibition Ground
- The Gabba, Brisbane, Queensland
- Manuka Oval, Canberra
- Melbourne Cricket Ground (MCG)
- Queen Elizabeth Oval, Bendigo
- Sydney Cricket Ground (SCG)
- Western Australian Cricket Association (WACA) Ground

BANGLADESH

- Sher-e-Bangla National Cricket Stadium (Mirpur Stadium), Mirpur

... Grounds continued

INDIA

- Eden Gardens, Kolkata
- Punjab Cricket Association Stadium, Mohali

NEW ZEALAND

- Basin Reserve (The Basin), Wellington
- Eden Park, Auckland
- McLean Park, Napier
- Seddon Park, Hamilton

SOUTH AFRICA

- Centurion Park, Centurion
- Kingsmead, Durban
- Old Wanderers, Johannesburg

UNITED ARAB EMIRATES

- Dubai International Cricket Stadium, Dubai

UK

- Headingley, Leeds
- Lord's, London
- The Oval (Kennington Oval), London
- Trent Bridge, Nottingham
- Old Trafford, Manchester

WEST INDIES

- Kensington Oval, Bridgetown, Barbados
- Windsor Park, Roseau, Dominica

Sam Anderson scored an estimated 100 career centuries.

George Bonnor, the Colonial Hercules.

Martin Bedkober died, aged 22, after being struck over the heart in a Brisbane club match in 1975.

Peggie Antonio, The Girl Grimmett.

Paying homage to a hero. Scott Boland's primary school, St John Vianney's, rejoiced in their famous old boy's fairytale Ashes debut.

Keith Jansz

Pictured with his younger brother Nick Boland (left) and Shane Warne, as a teenager Scott weighed more than 115 kg (18-plus stone). He still answers to the nickname of 'Barrel'.

Boland family archives

Scott's Johnny Mullagh Medal.

Boland's new celebrity status has seen him become an in-demand after-dinner speaker.

Australian Cricket Society

'Bush Bradman' Cec Pepper (pictured right) once hit a cricket ball 165 yards (150 metres) at Woodward Park in Parkes in the mid-'30s. Batting at the southern end, the ball steepled clear of the pickets, the parked cars and the tennis courts and finished in Victoria Street outside the Showground gates.

Artwork: Bruce Godden

Jeff Scotland scored 76 from 29 balls for the Australian Cricket Society's Over 60s at Kyabram in March 2022. The opposition demanded to see his birth certificate.

Peter Glenton

Dorothy Mort, the woman accused of shooting rising Australian batting star Claude Tozer, in 1920.

The Dave Sherwood memorial plaque at Coogee Oval. Sherwood was Randwick's first-grade scorer for 52 years and went on multiple tours with Australian Ashes teams.

Lyall Gardner

A cavorting Shane Warne at Trent Bridge after Australia won the Ashes in 1997.

Patrick Eagar/Ken Piesse collection/*Australian Cricket* magazine

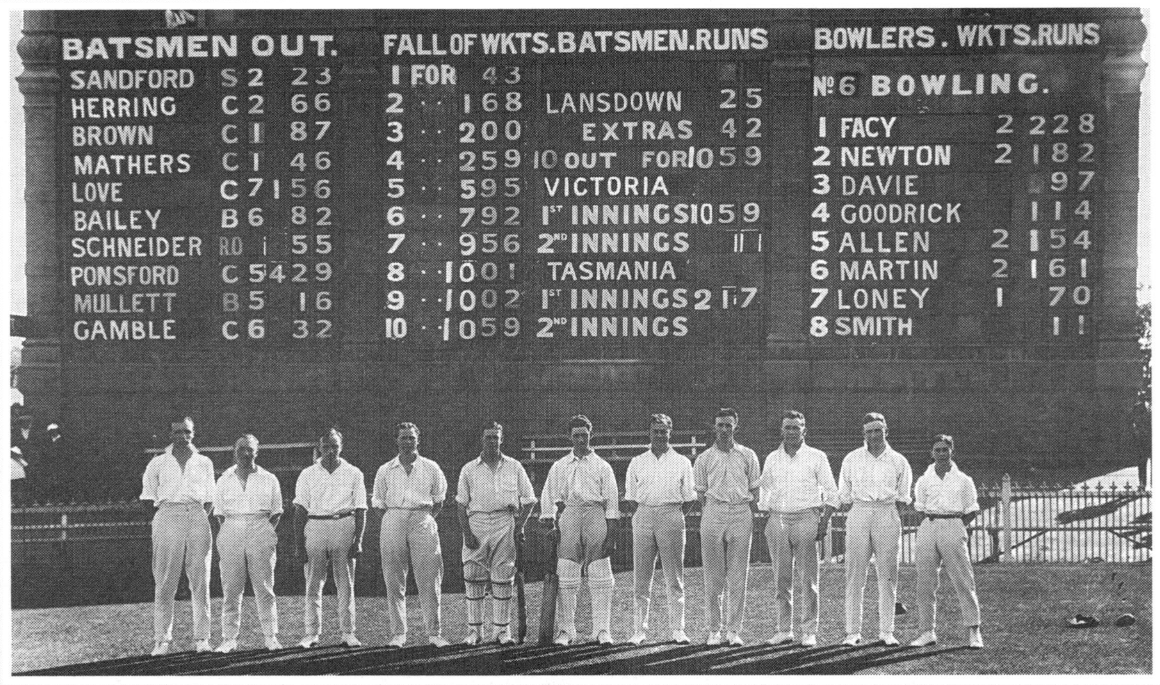

Bob Herring, brother of the celebrated Sir Edmund, opened for Victoria in the February 1923 MCG encounter against an understrength Tasmanian XI and scored 66 in a record four-figure score of 1059. Bill Ponsford made 429. Seven of the XI were making their Victorian debut. The team, from left to right: Bert Gamble, Bert Lansdown, Bill Bailey, Bert Brown, Ponsford, Hammy Love, Horace Sandford, Len Mullett, Jim Mathers, Herring and Karl Schneider.

Hall to Hurst

Wes Hall Was Australian club cricket's highest profile import at Randwick, NSW, in the '60s.

Jack Harry Endured the most sweltering conditions imaginable – 38 to 43°C (100 to 110°F) heat each and every day – in his one Test match, in Adelaide in high summer 1895. At 37, he is destined to remain the oldest of all of Australia's 72 'one-Test wonders'.

Roger Hartigan One of the select few to make a century on his Test debut, he also played cricket, baseball and lacrosse at interstate level and served on the Australian Cricket Board of Control for more than three decades. Was a prime mover in Brisbane, hosting international matches regularly from the late 1920s.

Neil Harvey The youngest of Don Bradman's Invincibles, he was never stumped in 137 Test innings.

Lindsay Hassett As a 17-year-old schoolboy at Geelong College, he made 147 not out against the touring West Indies. Included was 17 runs from one six-ball over from noted expressman Learie Constantine at Corio Oval, 1931.

Tom Hastings The first number 11 to make a Sheffield Shield century: Victoria vs South Australia, Melbourne, January 1903.

Bob Hawke The cricket-loving prime minister-to-be top scored with 39 against an array of Australian Test bowlers at a charity match in Sydney, October 1975. 'They went easy on me,' he was to say.

Matthew Hayden Made six hundreds in seven Boxing Day Test matches at the MCG between 2001 and 2007.

Marty Haywood Hit Wayne Mulherin for six sixes in an over: Randwick vs Petersham, Petersham Oval, 1993–94. Mulherin's figures blew out to none for 138 from 18 overs.

Alyssa Healy Almost single-handedly won Australia the 2022 50-over World Cup with a career-best 170 from 138 balls against old foes England at Hagley Oval, Christchurch. She hit 26 fours. Her husband, Test fast bowler Mitchell Starc, was an eyewitness, having just returned from an autumn-time tour of Pakistan. Healy also scored 129 in the semifinal.

Alyssa's celebrated uncle, Ian, was named the wicketkeeper in Australia's Team of the Century in 2000.

Sir Edmund Herring An ardent cricketer who was once bowled for a duck by WG Grace while representing 20 of Ballarat against Lord Sheffield's team, he was one of the great Australians of his generation, a Rhodes Scholar, a war hero, a Chief Justice and Lieutenant-Governor of Victoria.

His brother Bob played in the famous game in which Victoria amassed a first-class record score of 1059 against Tasmania at the MCG in 1922–23.

Neil Hicks Unhappy at play resuming against his wishes while it was raining, he took an umbrella out with him to ward off the elements: Mornington vs Seaford, Mornington Peninsula, 1970s.

Jim Higgs A perennial number 11, he was castled by the only ball he faced during the entire 1975 Ashes tour of England. Earlier that game, at Leicester, he was no-balled for deliberately throwing. He once did bat in the first four – for the Kyabram (Victoria) Fire Brigade.

Dot & Rex Higman The first husband and wife combination to umpire in Sydney grade cricket, in the 1970s.

Clem Hill Was involved in an infamous brawl with his chairman of selectors, Peter McAlister, upstairs at NSW cricket headquarters at Bulls Chambers in Martin Place, Sydney, in 1912. *See* Nervous Nineties

Denis Hill Took a wicket in the first over in his first six A grade games with Randwick, Sydney, as a teenager in 1967–68. His victims, in order, were Tony Steele, Ron Moroney, Bruce Francis, Ron Neill, Graham Southwell and Alan Crompton.

The Hill The vast expanse of grass (now the Trumper Stand) was home to the rowdiest and most raucous supporters in front of the old scoreboard at the Sydney Cricket Ground.

Mick Hinman The 11-year-old wrist-spinning prodigy from Maitland, NSW, took 132 C grade wickets for Louth Park including 14 in the 1931–32 final. He was presented with Clarrie Grimmett's book, *Getting Wickets*.

He later played in a NSW Second XI alongside emerging Test players, fellow teen Arthur Morris and Ron Saggers. He took a 'five-for' for Northern NSW

against Walter Hammond's 1946–47 English tourists in Newcastle. In 1949–50 he amassed a Maitland record 94 A grade wickets for Centrals.

Brad Hodge In Year 12 at St Bede's, he struck a ball over the cyclone fence at cover and into the Mentone Hotel, an extraordinary hit for anyone, let alone a 16-year-old schoolboy. Was rising 40 when he represented Australia for the last time in a Twenty20 international in Mirpur, Bangladesh, in 2014.

Rodney Hogg Avoided eating local food on his first tour to India in 1979, instead dining exclusively on cans of Heinz baked beans and spaghetti. Having bowled 21 no balls in the first Test and 21 in the second, he says he has never had even one baked bean since.

One of his many early jobs was as a milkman in Adelaide, before he was moved on, having missed a shift. Is now an acclaimed after-dinner speaker and raconteur.

Michael Holding During a stint as a professional with Tasmania, a nick flew wide of second slip to the fence.

'Captain,' called Mikey. 'Let's put a fieldsman there.'

'No, the horse has bolted.'

'There will be more horses.'

Darrell Holt Having umpired Shane Warne's third First XI game at Princes Park in January 1990, Holt was chatting with national selector and ex-Test leggie Jim Higgs outside the Victorian CA offices in Jolimont.

'This young fella turns it more than you, Jim,' said Holt.

'Rubbish.'

'He does . . . you'd better take a look at him. He's special.'

Higgs duly attended St Kilda's Thursday night club practice and, the next morning, 20-year-old Warne was added to Victoria's State practice squad. Within a month, he was playing first-class cricket.

Harold Hook Took 10 wickets and made 120 in the same match: Dollar vs Mirboo, South Gippsland, 1947–48.

Hal Hooker One of two Australians to take four wickets in four balls, in this case spread over two innings for NSW vs Victoria, Sydney 1928; a feat also achieved in 1965–66 by South Australia's Donn Robins.

David Hookes His blazing century from 34 balls remains the fastest in Sheffield Shield history. Angry at Victoria's delayed declaration, he'd promoted himself to opener and smashed 102 of a 120-run opening stand in less than an hour. His partner, Rick Darling, made 10.

'I've been watching cricket since 1919 and I have never seen anything like it,' said eyewitness and ex-Test batsman Len Darling.

Inside the rooms, receiving treatment for a torn hamstring, Victoria's Peter Cox wondered if it was hailing outside, there were so many 'bangs' on the tin roof – all the result of Hookes's pyrotechnics. At the height of his onslaught, rookie Victorian Peter King conceded 38 runs from two overs in Adelaide, October 1982.

James Hopes With almost 100 appearances, Hopes remains the most capped Australian white-ball cricketer of all not to play Tests.

Tom Horan The first bowler in Ashes history to hit the stumps with his very first delivery. It came in his tenth Test in Sydney 1883. (The next to do it was Shane Warne, in 1993.)

Wally Horne Lifted Marrickville to a famous first-ever Sydney first-grade title by striking Bill (Tiger) O'Reilly over cow corner for six in the very final over of the Grand Final: Marrickville vs St George, Sydney, April 1944.

Eric Horsted The Irrewillipe dairy farmer made 20 centuries in and around Colac, Victoria, despite an artificial left leg. Once he was run out on 99 after his leg fell off as he was coming back for two.

Jack House The curator responsible for illegally watering the Melbourne pitch in heatwave conditions on the Sunday of the crucial third Test (the series was tied at 1–1). Eyeing a dry, cracked MCG wicket, he said, 'Someone will get killed out here. I'm gonna give it a fizz.' He saturated the entire square, leading to a world scoop for *The Age*'s cricket writer Percy Beames, who had been tipped off by a member of the ground staff, one of Beames's old football teammates; January 1955.

Howard Houston His service to leading Melbourne club Carlton as player and administrator spanned 66 years.

John Howard On his way to becoming prime minister, he shouted each of his West Pennant Hills cricket teammates a carton of beer for letterboxing his electorate in the early '70s. In 12 years of Saturday club cricket Howard averaged 20 runs a season and failed to take a wicket.

Kim Hughes The first to hit sixes on all five days of a Test match: Australia vs England, Centenary Test, Lord's, August–September 1980.

Tom Hume Took eight for 0 from four maiden overs for Waverley College Under 13s at Barker College in 1993. The Barker boys were all out for one, their solitary run a bye. Asked about his feat, Hume later said, 'I thought they were saving their best batsmen until last.' The match was over in half an hour.

Bill Hunt A one-Tester whose fruity language dismayed many in authority, Hunt took six wickets and two hat-tricks in an over on the eve of the 1936–37 Sydney first-grade cricket season: Balmain vs Rydalmere. His analysis was WWW•WWW•. Seventy of his 203 eight-ball overs that club season were maidens.

Alan Hurst The first to make six ducks in an Ashes series in 1978–79.

Ingwersen to Ivory

Alec Ingwersen Took 11 for 32 when Ferntree Gully played Yea and District in a one-innings game on malthoid in early summer 1965. The home team was none for 82 before Ingwersen brought himself on at third change and took his first wicket with his right-arm medium pace swingers. Seven of his wickets were bowled, two lbw and two caught. Both teams batted 12.

'I gave the quicker blokes a go first,' Ingwersen said. 'I took the first 10 and the last wicket was this six-foot-ten fella [K Oliver, 208 centimetres]. I hit him high above the knee roll and Noel Moore, the umpire, said "That's close enough," and gave him out lb!'

John Inverarity Australia's selection chairman responsible for Ashton Agar's shock first Test selection in the opening Ashes Test of 2013 at Trent Bridge. Selected primarily as a left-arm finger spinner, Agar scored an even-time 98, from number 11. Noted for his integrity, leadership, skill and professionalism, there has been no more important figure in the history of Western Australian cricket than Inverarity.

The Invincibles The famous epithet for Don Bradman's 'Greats of '48', unbeaten through all 34 touring matches. Having turned 40 late in the campaign, Bradman averaged 90 for the tour and 72 in the Tests. 'He was unbelievably good then,' said 19-year-old Neil Harvey. 'He must have been extraordinary before the war.'

Frank Iredale The first Ashes batsman to be run out going for a five at Kennington Oval, 1896. Was witness to the famous fistfight between his fellow selectors,

Test captain Clem Hill and Peter McAlister, in Sydney in February 1912.

Bert Ironmonger Australia's oldest Test cricketer at 51. Assisted Don Bradman to his only century of the Bodyline series. The Don was on 97 when Bert ambled in at number 11 in Melbourne, January 1933.

'I won't let you down son,' he said. Having survived the last two balls of an over, he watched with satisfaction as Bradman duly reached his century in the very next over with a fierce pull shot through midwicket.

Ironmonger was denied the opportunity to tour England in 1934, his action being considered 'jerky' and his occupation – a lawnmowing man for St Kilda Council – unsuitable, given the team's numerous social engagements. All 14 of his Test matches were in Australia. *See* Dolly

Jack Iverson Described once as the least accomplished and most uncoordinated cricketer to play Ashes cricket, Big Jake couldn't bat, preferred to field with his feet and often felt inadequate alongside the likes of Morris, Miller and co. But his confounding each-way spin and uninhibited, kangaroo-hopping celebrations on taking a wicket ensured his Australia-wide popularity.

Flicking the ball from a bent middle finger, he was a revelation from the time he took 15 wickets in a day on debut with Brighton's Third XI in Victoria in 1946, and was immediately promoted to the firsts.

He embarrassed countless batting lineups on his way to Test selection just four years later. In newsreel footage of his bowling action, his bowling hand was deliberately 'blacked out' so Freddie Brown's 1950–51 Englishmen could not better decipher his mysteries. 'Jack had no idea just how good he was,' said teammate Colin McDonald.

Iverson's fragile self-confidence hastened his sudden exit from big-time cricket. He returned to Brighton Beach where he continued to dominate, taking 141 First XI wickets in two seasons in his late forties. He also toured India with a Commonwealth team where one of his wickets came with an underarm.

Wilfred Ivory Called up at the eleventh hour to represent The Rest vs An Australian XI for Tommy Warne's testimonial, in Melbourne in 1911, he took two stumpings and made a duck in his only first-class appearance.

Jacobs to Junor

The Reverend Garry Jacobs When it was learned that the newly appointed Presbyterian Church minister at bayside Beaumaris, Melbourne, also kept wickets and batted high, Jacobs was immediately enlisted in the local First XI. One early-season club Saturday, rising teenager John Ward was having little luck. Jacobs kept beating the outside edge and the batsman responded with colourful insults and oaths in the fruitiest possible language.

'John, John,' called the Rev. 'Never, ever use Christ's name in vain.'

'Sorry Rev, sorry,' said Ward.

Next over, the batsman finally nicked one straight to Jacobs who inexplicably grassed the catch. 'You bastard,' said the Rev, throwing a fist at the sky. 'Where were you when I bloody well needed you?'

Ivan James The Timaru (NZ) chemist helped revive Richie Benaud's bowling career by prescribing a lotion that repaired his bloodied spinning finger and triggered a set of dominant performances home and away. The miracle lotion was a combination of an oily calamine lotion and boracic acid powder. 'It saved my career,' said Benaud.

Barry Jarman Australia's most travelled reserve wicketkeeper, he wore his baggy green almost 100 times through eight tours. Just 19 of the matches, however, were Tests, but in one he was stand-in captain.

One of his most satisfying seasons was his last, as mentor and playing coach for the Kensington Under 16s in Adelaide in 1977, local rules having been changed to allow one senior to be on the field with the teenagers.

J

Don Jeffery The Sydney banker took eight catches in the field in a match in Rabaul (Papua New Guinea) in 1972–73. The first two were in the covers and the rest at cow corner.

Wayne Jenkin In October 1976, he made himself unavailable for selection for St Kilda's Fourth XI due to a clash with ballroom dancing lessons.

Terry Jenner Was on parole when he met Shane Warne, whom he was to coach throughout his stellar career. He'd earlier been sentenced to six-and-a-half years jail for embezzlement, Judge Greaves calling him a 'parasite' and 'a pathological gambler'. *See* Rohan Kanhai

Ian Johnson Fielded and bowled in his first post-war Ashes Tests without socks, in 1946–47.

Len Johnson On the very day the most famous touring team of all was announced, Don Bradman's 1948 Ashes 17, Len 'the Lionheart' Johnson from far north Rockhampton took six wickets for 26 runs against India at the MCG – and still missed selection.

Bill Johnston The number 11 averaged 102 on Australia's 1953 Coronation Year tour, going undismissed in 16 of his 17 first-class innings. Delighted at his rare milestone, he said it didn't come as a great personal surprise: 'You know, I did used to bat at number four for Beeac High School.' Originally from a farm at Ondit.

Rod Johnston The first from Broken Hill to play four 'bush internationals' in the '80s, he was also a member of South Australia's Combined Country XIs on eight occasions, four times as captain.

Ernie Jones Once sent a ball through Dr WG Grace's famed beard.

Ray Jordon Short and squat in stature, even his own family called him The Slug. Toured as reserve wicketkeeper with Bill Lawry's Australians in 1969–70 to Ceylon (Sri Lanka), India and South Africa without playing a Test.

Brendon Julian The first cricketer of Polynesian descent to represent Australia, he moved with his family from his native New Zealand to Port Hedland at seven, then on to Perth where he attended one of the great cricket schools, Guildford Grammar.

Later he became the face of Fox Cricket after the death of David Hookes.

Len Junor In 1930, he became the youngest Australian first-class cricketer at 15 years and 265 days. He was also among the shortest cricketers, at 162 centimetres (five foot four).

kamahl to korumburra

Kamahl Bowled handy off breaks in the lower grades in the '60s with Kensington CC, Don Bradman's club. The Don loved to talk music while Kamahl was always slanting the conversation back to cricket.

At the launch of my Boys' Own annual *Our Don Bradman* in 2008, Kamahl sang 'Ol' Man River', one of the Don's all-time favourites from *Show Boat*.

He told the story of the Don marvelling at the voice of Paul Robeson when he and Lady Jessie saw *Show Boat* live on Broadway during their extended playing honeymoon to the United States in 1932. Kamahl's rendition in the Windsor Hotel's ornate ballroom triggered prolonged applause from all. Also in the room were Arthur and Judy Morris and the Don's son, John.

Kamikaze Kids The unflattering nickname given to rookie openers Rick Darling and Graeme Wood after a series of mix-ups running between the wickets in the 1978–79 Ashes series. Australia had never selected a younger opening pair.

Rohan Kanhai The West Indian champion was a regular visitor to Australia in the '60s and '70s. In Perth for a semi-successful season of Sheffield Shield in 1961–62, he was at the WACA nets and pasting all comers; in particular, squad rookie Terry Jenner's flighty wrist spinners. Later he told TJ that he was signalling his wrong 'un with a cocked little finger. A decade later in Trinidad, Jenner bowled Kanhai with a googly in a Test match. It was among the most satisfying wickets of his career.

Tom Kendall Bowled from just two paces. Took seven wickets in England's second innings in the inaugural Test match in Melbourne, March 1877.

Alex Kermode Chosen directly from Moore Park juniors to represent New South Wales, he took five wickets in his only Sheffield Shield game in Sydney, January 1902.

AB (Bev) Kerrigan Captaining Trinity Grammar in a school match, in Sydney, 1916, he was feeling rather pleased with himself, having struck seven boundaries in the final over before lunch, only to be told by coach Archie Ferrier, 'Calm down you bloody fool, or they'll take him [the bowler] off.'

Ian Kevan Mike Hussey's acclaimed coach.

Ian King In 1969–70, he became the first Indigenous fast bowler to play at first-class level since fellow Queenslander Eddie Gilbert in the late 1930s.

John Kinloch The last of the underarmers, the first nightwatchman and the first to 'Mankad' an opponent, he captained the NSW XXII that opposed HH Stephenson's touring Englishmen in early 1862.

Joe Kinnear Worked the old scoreboard at the Melbourne Cricket Ground from 1932 until his retirement in 1977, when he was 65.

Maree Kinniburgh Having moved to Welshpool in the '70s, she became the first full-time women's player in South Gippsland, among her feats being her debut match dismissal of Tarwin's B grade captain Jim Doyle for a golden duck. She also won the club's bowling averages in 1981–82.

Jack Kirby Scored 15,000 runs (with 33 hundreds) for North Balwyn CC in 395 games stretching over four decades to the mid-'80s in Melbourne's Eastern Cricket Association competition. Won the club's batting average 22 times.

The Reverend Wallace Kirkby Gave seven lbw decisions in one innings in the Sydney lower grades one day in the late '60s. When queried, he said, 'Had the fielding team appealed for two more decisions I would have given those as well.'

Lindsay Kline Took a rare Test hat-trick and, from number 11, batted 110 minutes for the 15 of his life to help save a Test match: Australia vs West Indies, Adelaide, February 1961.

Clarice Knight Was the long-time scoreboard operator at the NTCA Ground in Launceston. On leaving, in 1949, after more than 20 years of continuous service at pennant and international games, she received a silver tea set.

Korumburra Serenaders Played the music at the premiership celebrations for Milford CC at the Dumbalk North Hall on 3 June, 1936. Mr Bob Patterson was engaged for 10 shillings to take a bus load to the ball. Admission was gents, three shillings, and ladies, one shilling and sixpence. Caterers were Tobias and Considine.

L

Labuschagne to Ludwig

Marnus Labuschagne Before becoming cricket's first concussion sub (Lord's 2019), he featured three times on international scorecards before making his first runs in Test cricket.

As a substitute fieldsman, he took a catch against India in his hometown Brisbane (2014). On his Test debut in Dubai (2018), he ran out Pakistan's rising champion Babar Azam and, with his sliding leg breaks, dismissed Asad Shafiq for 80.

Bruce Laird Possessed the stoutest defence of any Australian opening batsman. Was dismissed 'bowled' just once in 38 Test innings.

Peter Landers Miffed at being demoted to the Third XI at St Joseph's, Geelong, Pete was out for a blob, right on tea-time, lbw to one which struck him around the navel. Furiously throwing his gear into his car, he drove at speed onto the club's Carey Oval, upending cones and demolishing both sets of stumps and continuing straight out the main gate. His St Joey mates still describe it as the greatest straight drive ever seen on the Surf Coast. They found him much, much later at a local watering hole, still in his whites and still with his head in his hands, bemoaning the injustice of it all.

Dot Laughton Australian women's oldest Test debutante at 35. Scored 47 against England at the SCG. It was to be her only appearance, in February 1949.

Jack Laver Took one of the greatest return catches ever seen at the NTCA ground when he caught and bowled the West Indian Denis Atkinson for 19 on his way to four for 81 in Launceston, January 1952. His uncle was Golden Age great Frank Laver.

Stuart Law Only the second Australian, after Don Bradman, to make more than 100 representative hundreds. Yet he played just one Test.

Bill Lawry Famously dubbed 'the corpse with pads on' by noted English writer Ian Wooldridge in London's *Daily Mail* during yet another laborious Ashes innings – 94 in five-plus hours at the Oval in 1964.

Brett Lee Recorded the fastest timed delivery by an Australian: 160.8 kilometres per hour (99.92 mph) at Napier (NZ) in 2005.

Ian Lee At 13, he remains the youngest ever First XI player at Melbourne District/Premier League level: South Melbourne vs Carlton, 1927–28.

In Sydney, Graham Southwell was 14 when he made his First XI debut for Northern District against Glebe in 1952–53. The youngest South Australian First XI player was CF Whitridge for Norwood, in 1874–75. He also was 14.

John Leehane This Victorian fast bowler of the late '70s had one of the great nicknames: Luna, short for 'lunatic'.

Mick Lewis His analysis of 10–0–113–0 is the most expensive in Australian ODIs: Australia vs South Africa, Johannesburg, March 2006. He never played for Australia again.

Gary Lidgerwood Dismissed champion West Indian Desmond Haynes, for 0 and one, in back-to-back bush internationals in the early '80s. 'You grasped the opportunity to rub shoulders with some of the greats of the game,' he said. 'Good crowds turned up and there was a buzz around town [Wangaratta] for weeks before and after. Unfortunately, there's not enough room in the schedule these days.'

Greg Lill The first to umpire 400 first-grade games in Sydney. Umpired at the top level from 1989 to 2016. Remains a salt-of-the-earth mentor in the lower grades to new match officials.

Dennis Lillee Asked Queen Elizabeth for her autograph when she met the two teams during the Centenary Test in Melbourne in 1977. Her Majesty later granted Lillee his request, via the post. Used an aluminium bat in two Tests (1979–80) and bowled a tennis ball in a county match in England in 1972.

His first Western Australian captain Tony Lock dubbed him FOT (Flippin' Ol' Tart, or something like that).

Lilli'an Thomson Australia's quickest and most destructive new-ball combo of them all who piloted Australia's rise to world champion status in the mid-'70s.

Linton Ling After having his right arm severed just below the elbow in an industrial accident, Linton resumed his cricket career with Geelong City in 1973–74, batting with one hand and a hook. He taught himself to bowl left-arm finger spin and was thrice City's

Club Champion. His son, Cameron, won fame as an AFL premiership captain at Geelong FC.

Tommy Lloyd Taker of 2500 career wickets in the Western Districts of Victoria, including 100 in 1967–68, he played to a ripe old age before turning to lawn bowls. Asked if he was enjoying his second sport, he said, 'Yes, it's okay.'

'Is it as good as cricket?'

'Nothing is as good as cricket and I mean nothing!'

Tony Lock Forced to run a 'five' by his younger and fitter partner Ian Brayshaw, at the MCG in November 1965, the old English Test cricketer met his teammate mid-pitch and declared: 'Never do that to me again, son.'

Martin Love Scored a record 10,532 runs across 11 seasons before first playing for Australia. Was dropped after making a century against Bangladesh in a rare wintertime Test, in Cairns in 2003.

Ron Lovitt Snapped cricket's quintessential photograph for the Melbourne *Age* of Joe Solomon's run out of Ian Meckiff in Test cricket's most famous finish. The match was tied with both teams scoring 734 runs, over five fabulous days in Brisbane, December 1960.

Annie Loxton Her freshly cut cucumber sandwiches were famous all around Melbourne among Saturday afternoon cricketers sampling afternoon tea at Toorak Park; before and well after World War II. Like Sam, senior and junior, she was accorded life membership at Prahran CC.

John Loxton He was dismissed for 99 on debut, a score later altered to 100 after it was found one of his runs had been mistakenly given to teammate Bob Crane: Queensland vs Western Australia, WACA Ground, December 1966.

Sam Loxton The last Australian team manager to play a first-class match, aged 38, during Australia's tour of India when others were ill and unavailable. Opposing the Combined Indian Universities at Bangalore's Central College ground, he made 32 (from number five) and took none for 32 (opening the bowling alongside Alan Davidson) in January 1960.

Alan Ludwig Took a hat-trick from the first three balls of the match: Army vs Logan Village, Beenleigh, Queensland, 1946.

LAUGHTER IS THE BEST MEDICINE

Having bought a raffle ticket in the main street in Perth, Andrew Symonds asked, 'When will it be drawn?'

'The 31st.'

'Okay, I'll see you on the 32nd.'

———

Lismore's Andrew Cartledge was feeling decidedly dusty on Day Two of a Saturday–Sunday match against Woorndoo. Within minutes of being run out for a diamond duck, he vomited all over his whites before being pooped on by a seagull through the open window of a mate's ute, in 2005.

———

A six-hit from Toombul's Kent Officer catapulted out of Bottomley Park (now Peter Burge Oval) and skipped down a nearby road. Westies captain John Salter was at long on and had to open a side gate and head down the road to retrieve it. So far away did the ball finish that a local resident mowing his lawn said, 'Gee mate, is there a cricket ground around here?' *Brisbane First XI club cricket, mid–'80s.*

———

The ball soared over the fence and into the Royal Prince Alfred Hospital. It was a huge, steepling hit. Sydney Uni's Craig Tomko gingerly mastered the cyclone wire fence into the hospital grounds, retrieved the ball and slowly retraced his return to the centre pitch with the ball cupped lovingly in his hands.

'Take care of that ball,' he said. 'It has had six stitches.' *Sydney University vs Penrith, December 1981.*

———

... Laughter is the best medicine continued

Passing Royal Randwick one day on the way to the Sydney Cricket Ground, Australia's new white-ball spinner Brad Hogg innocently asked, 'Is that where they hold the Melbourne Cup?'

— — —

Victor Profitt was among Geelong's best Saturday afternoon allrounders. One Saturday he arrived back home triumphant.

'Darling,' he said. 'I've done it'.

'What?'

'100 wickets and 1000 runs.'

'You must be exhausted. Come and have a cuppa.'

— — —

Lindsay Hassett was normally eloquent and occasionally loquacious in his expert comments role on ABC radio. One day, though, referring to a stand between Queenslanders Peter Burge and Ken Mackay, he called it 'a fine farting partnership'.
See Tall Stories & True

— — —

Kerrigundi's Theo White was at the crease when struck by a short ball which ignited a box of wax matches he was carrying in his hip pocket. To the merriment of those around him he had to roll on his side to douse the flames. *Cobar Association, 1950s.*

— — —

During one of his many trips to England, Arthur Mailey was at a country estate party when he was asked by the hostess, who knew nothing about cricket, if he'd care to dance.

'No Ma'am,' he replied. 'I'm a little stiff from bowling.'

'Oh,' she said, 'Is that where you come from?'

MacGill to Musgrove

Stuart MacGill Possessed the best wrong 'un in the game, far superior to even Shane Warne's. In 16 Tests together, MacGill took 82 wickets at 22 and Warne took 74 at 29.

JRM (Sunny Jim) Mackay His spectacular clean hitting was the feature of an extraordinary Sydney first-grade opening stand of 309 in 87 minutes with Austin Diamond for Burwood (later Western Suburbs) against Middle Harbour at Manly in the mid-1900s. In making 156 not out, Mackay hit eight 'fives' including a colossal on-drive which landed on the balcony of a house on the hill at the northern end, 55 metres outside the ground. Another, also at the northern end, soared over the big fig tree and yet another struck the Presbyterian manse 45 metres from the ground. All his biggest hits came against first-year bosie bowler Jimmy Randell. The season of his life came immediately after he'd missed selection for the 1905 Ashes tour: Mackay made 1041 runs at an average of 100-plus for club and 559 at 111 for NSW. Only Victor Trumper attracted larger crowds to Sydney club matches.

Ken Mackay Led the Australians from the field at Kennington Oval in 1961, having bowled a marathon 107 overs for the match. 'Richie ... thank you,' he said to his captain Richie Benaud. 'I've bowled more overs this Test than Ian Johnson gave me for the whole tour in '56.' Years earlier, as a Brisbane schoolboy, he'd made 367 not out and taken all 10 wickets in an innings: Virginia vs Sherwood, 1939–40.

Ian Maddocks In an era of ultraconservative administration, few sponsorships and all-white uniforms, Maddocks was forced to change his coloured batting gloves during a First XI match at North Melbourne in 1975.

Jimmy Maher Scored an unequalled 50 centuries as a teenager in and around Cairns. His first hundred came at the age of nine.

Arthur Mailey The most whimsical of cricketers and critics, he once selected an English Test XI without a wicketkeeper, in Brisbane, December 1950.

'They won't need one,' said Mailey. 'They won't get a ball past the bat.'

George Major Was enlisted to select a new Australian XI for the New Year Test of 1885 in Melbourne after a player rebellion. Nine were new to Test cricket. Five never played again.

Ashley Mallett Among the few Australian off-spinners to take 100 Test wickets, he was once struck for five consecutive sixes by the South African Mike Procter in a game against Western Province, at Newlands, Cape Town in 1970. 'Well, Rowd,' said Doug Walters. 'That's got rid of the reds. Now we're onto the coloured balls.'

Alec Marks A pleasant Sunday afternoon's boating on the Hawkesbury almost turned to tragedy when Marks playfully pushed his NSW teammate, young recordholder Don Bradman, into the river, 90 metres off the pier at Berowra. The young Don was spluttering and about to go under for the second time when Jessie Bradman, from the wharf, screamed, 'Grab him Acka [Marks], grab him. He can't swim!' Marks duly pulled him back into the boat and saved Bradman's life.

Ron Marks Made a 24-ball century for Woongoolba in the Beenleigh–Logan area of Queensland in 1940.

Jack Marsh The first great Indigenous fast bowler was denied higher honours by prejudice and bigoted thinking. He was also a champion sprinter, the fastest in Australia. 'Marsh was never allowed the chance to find out how good he really was,' said his biographer Max Bonnell.

Rod Marsh After his underwhelming debut Test (1970–71), when he replaced eastern states favourite Brian Taber and was dubbed Iron Gloves, Marsh deliberately squashed the favourite hat of one of his fiercest critics, Jack Fingleton, in the plane's overhead locker on the flight out of Brisbane.

Jim (Snakey) Marshall Once bowled Don Bradman for a golden duck, but as it was a 'trial ball' (allowed at the time), the young Don stayed and top-scored with 31 in 15 minutes: Railway vs Butter Factory, Carrington Park, Casino, NSW, April 1929.

Geoff Martin Was bowled by England's expressman Harold Larwood one day, the bail landing 68 yards (62 metres) away in Launceston, January 1929.

Jack Martin The best number eight in Mirboo CC's history, renowned for his big hits, he'd wear only one pad

and would drop one of his braces straps off his shoulder to allow his right arm more freedom to swing. When the club moved from its ground on the Tarwin River in Victoria to a sheep paddock abutting the local hotel, big Jack launched a huge steepler into the beer garden. It skipped along the verandah and rolled straight into the back bar. Play stopped for half an hour as the ball was retrieved and many celebratory frothies downed in Jack's honour.

EJ (Teddy) Martin The first Australian first-class cricketer to live to the age of 100.

Johnnie Martin The left-arm spinning debutant from Burrell Creek, NSW, dismissed the champion West Indian trio of Garry Sobers, Rohan Kanhai and Frank Worrell in four balls, in Melbourne, 1961. A big hitter in the middle order, his 166 sixes is a long-time club record at Petersham–Marrickville, NSW.

Damien Martyn Averaged 104 on the 2001 tour of England; the best since Don Bradman's 115 in 1938.

Jimmy Matthews Took two Test hat-tricks on the same afternoon: Australia vs South Africa, Old Trafford, May 1912.

Tim May Recorded a 52-ball, 64-minute duck, the longest in Australian first-class cricket, to help South Australia force a draw to ensure the 1995–96 Sheffield Shield title in Adelaide. Teammate and captain Jamie Siddons stonewalled for even longer: 166 minutes for four runs.

Jack McAuliffe Was out without scoring, having batted for 22 eight-ball overs: Bruton vs Fairy Hill, Casino, NSW, 1932–33.

Stan McCabe Scored 72 of a 77-run tenth wicket stand with LO'B (Chuck) Fleetwood-Smith on his way to an epic 232: Australia vs England, first Test, Trent Bridge, June 1938. Don Bradman shook his hand in the rooms, telling McCabe, 'I'd give a great deal to be able to play an innings like that.'

Colin McCool Took five wickets in five balls for Brisbane against North Coast at Gympie, in November 1947. Played 14 Tests without even one loss. Was still playing at A grade level in Newcastle in his mid-fifties.

Ernie McCormick Bowled 19 no balls in his first three overs at Worcester in the opening game of the 1938 Ashes tour. 'It's alright,' he said at lunch. 'The umpire is hoarse.' A silversmith by trade, he designed the original Frank Worrell Trophy, which went missing for years, having been stashed in an old wardrobe belonging to Dessie Haynes's grandmother in Barbados.

Rick McCosker Walked out to bat, his head swathed in bandages, on the Monday of the Centenary Test to choruses of 'Waltzin' McCosker, Waltzin' McCosker'. He'd had his jaw broken by Bob Willis on the first morning of the epic match in Melbourne, March 1977.

Colin McDonald Released his second autobiography *Taking Strike* in 2015 at the age of 87. Preferred to sign autographs with his left hand and write with his right.

In 1959 he was ranked the number one batsman in the world. Bill Brown loved his square cut.

In the days when the ABC radio commentators had to sit out in the open in the Melbourne Cricket Club's old cigar stand, his beach umbrella was always prominent.

Played his last five seasons with Brighton subbies, on the proviso that he not practise.

Ted McDonald Castled Don Bradman for nine in a tour match at Liverpool, UK, bowling with genuine pace despite being in his fortieth year. The Don rated the ex-Australian as one of the fastest and best bowlers he'd ever faced.

Percy McDonnell Scored 82 of an 86-run opening stand with the stonewalling Alick Bannerman against the North of England in Manchester in 1888.

Bryce McGain Always wanted to make a hundred for Australia; never dreamt it would come from his first 11½ overs, during his only Test match, in Cape Town, 2008. A late bloomer, he was still playing, aged 50, at Premier Fourth XI standard alongside son Liam in 2022.

Alan McGilvray The 'voice' of Australian cricket, the long-time commentary doyen famously missed the gripping final two hours of cricket's first tied Test (Brisbane 1960) when he – and Keith Miller – caught an early flight home to Sydney.

John McIlwraith The first to score consecutive first-class centuries in high summer 1885–86. Flopped in his only Test match.

Graham McKenzie Was nicknamed 'Garth' after the ageless post-war comic book superhero.

Rex McKenzie So fiery and threatening was The Dimboola Express one very grey midweek morning in Hamilton, Victoria, in 1965, that the MCC threatened to stop play. Ken Barrington walked in to bat with a message from captain Mike Smith: 'Take McKenzie off, or we're going off.'

Barrington later commended McKenzie on his disconcerting pace and asked him what he did for a living.

'I was an axeman,' he said. 'Now I work for the local shire [as a front-end loader driver].'

'You're a bloody fool,' Barrington said. 'You're wasting your time. You should come over to England and play.'

Max & Pixie McKiehan In the early '80s in Launceston, they became the only married couple to umpire first-grade cricket.

Charlie McLaughlin Walked unannounced into Randwick's Coogee Oval in Sydney on the Tuesday night before the opening game of 1938–39 and asked to have a bowl. He was shirtless and with his striking jet-black coiffed hair, deep tan and rippling Johnny Weissmuller physique, he looked like an Adonis. From seven paces he bowled like the wind and was included straight away in Randwick's First XI, attracting an immediate following, especially among the girls. And for several years he was the fastest bowler in all Sydney.

Doug McLean A chubby keeper and opening bat, he took eight catches, including the first seven in a row in a Melbourne District First XI semifinal: St Kilda vs Essendon, Junction Oval 1964–65.

John McMahon Rochester's all-round sporting champion scored 1100 runs and took 117 wickets in the 1969–70 season, becoming known as 'the man who never fails'. His daughter Sharelle was a world champion netballer.

Sir Robert Menzies Cajoled Sir Donald Bradman, 54, into playing one last 'international' in his 1962–63 Prime Minister's XI fixture against the touring English team at Manuka Oval. The Don made four.

Zdravko Micevic The bouncer acquitted of charges of manslaughter in the tragic death of David Hookes, 48, outside an inner-Melbourne bayside hotel in early 2004.

Billy Midwinter The first in Australian club cricket to score a double century, in 1869–70 in Bendigo. Originally from the Cotswolds, his family had moved to gold town Bendigo when young Billy was nine. Was to represent both Australia and England in Tests.

Colin Milburn The big-eating, beer-swilling 110 kilogram (17 stone 3 pounds) heavyweight from tiny Burnopfield in County Durham, UK, smashed an Australian session record 181 from 134 balls at the Gabba and was so exhausted at the tea break that he could barely lift himself from his chair to resume his innings: Western Australia vs Queensland, November 1968.

Reg Miles Smashed 44 from one eight-ball over and, later in the same season, 50. His sequence was 6666662nb66: Temora, March 1937.

Averaged 100 plus in five consecutive bush seasons with Springdale from 1933–34.

Helen Milford Served afternoon teas to the players for 60 years at Petersham–Marrickville and Randwick–Petersham cricket clubs.

Military Cricket Club The first cricket club in Australia, formed in 1826.

Colin Miller The first blue-haired bowler to take a Test wicket, West Indian number 11 Courtney Walsh, in Sydney 2001. On debut at Rawalpindi in 1998, Miller's hair colour was a Billy Idol white blond. He could bowl both fast and slow, *à la* the great Bill Johnston.

Grant Miller The Eden concreter took 10 for 29 and scored 42 not out in the Grand Final play-off before Bega–Angledale conceded the match at drinks on day two at George Griffin Oval, Eden, NSW, March 2006.

Keith Miller As a starstruck Melbourne teenager, he'd camp outside Bill Ponsford's house at number 24 Orrong Road, Elsternwick, hoping that the front door would open and Bill would come outside to play with the local kids. 'But he never did,' said Miller years later, 'not even once.'

Roy Miller Rated the finest Victorian bush cricketer of them all, among many laurels are his eight centuries

before lunch at Bendigo Country Week. Born in Barham and schooled at Koondrook and Kerang, his artistry, skill and sheer talent prompted Bill Woodfull to once say, 'If it wasn't for a paddock full of cows and a blue-eyed girl, he would have played for Australia.'

The Miracle Match The most electric early one-day game held on a lightning-fast wicket at the WACA Ground in December 1976, involving five of cricket's most distinguished: Greg Chappell, Dennis Lillee, Rod Marsh, Jeff Thomson and West Indian import Viv Richards.

After Western Australia made just 77, batting first in the Gillette Cup semifinal, Lillee spearheaded a remarkable comeback, dismissing Richards (0) and Chappell (2) as Queensland capitulated for 62. Coming back into cricket after back surgery, Lillee risked his whole career by bowling so fast. He was man of the match, with four for 21 from 7.3 of the most hostile overs he ever delivered.

'We all felt such a passion for Western Australia,' Lillee was to say. 'I would have died for the team.'

Clarence Moody The visionary 'father' of Test cricket, he suggested, in his book *Australian Cricket and Cricketers* (1894), a list of 'Test' matches which were to become accepted by authorities from both England and Australia, dating back to the first 'Grand Match', in Melbourne in 1877.

JFC Moore Made the largest recorded and measured hit of them all: 170 yards (155 metres), at Griffith in the

NSW southern Riverina, 1929–30. He is regarded as the Atlas of Australian country cricket.

Peter Morelli The biggest bush cricketer of all at 180 kilograms (nearly 30 stone). The Copabella train driver learned to play at Mt Carmel College in Charters Towers and regularly represented the Hughenden Mutts XI at the Goldfield and Reedybrook Ashes. At his size, he'd look to hit only fours and sixes with the occasional single. Twos and threes were never, ever contemplated.

Henry Morley Smashed 62 from one extended over from R Grubb: Tourists vs Gargett, Mackay, Queensland, 1968–69. The over blew out to 12 balls because of four no balls. Morley hit nine sixes and two fours.

Jack Moroney The only Australian opener to make a pair in his single Ashes Test in Brisbane, 1950.

Arthur Morris The old Bradman Invincible was asked once what he'd got out of cricket. 'Poverty,' he said.

Morwell River Prison XI Won the Mid-Gippsland A grade Premiership in its first year, 1961, under the captaincy of M Holt. More success was elusive. 'The problem with the River,' said spokesman Jim Williams, 'is that just when we get our act together, good players are released.'

Jeff Moss Among the elite to have averaged 60 in Test cricket, from just one match, against Pakistan; Perth 1978–79. Still answers to Groucho, for his full, bushy

eyebrows and moustache, reminiscent of the celebrated comedian Groucho Marx.

AG (Johnnie) Moyes One of the most prominent players, writers and commentators, among his 14 books was the first biography of Don Bradman, published in 1948. On Moyes's death in 1963, Bradman called his old mentor 'unique and irreplaceable'.

Pat Mullins The Brisbane solicitor was going blind so sold all of his 8000 cricket books, all double-stacked in bowing wooden bookcases at his home in suburban Coorparoo, to the Melbourne Cricket Club in 1988. At the height of the Brisbane floods in 1974, his children asked him which of his most treasured books would he try and save.

'I'd go down with all of them,' he said.

Nigel Murch Tall, tanned and blond, he dated celebrated English pop singer Dusty Springfield for three steamy months in 1968 during a stint with Northamptonshire. They'd met at a night club on the High Street. 'Would you like a dance?' he asked her between brackets.

'Yes.'

'Would you like to come home with me?'

'Yes.'

A fast bowler in two ofVictoria's Sheffield Shield winning seasons from the mid-'60s, he hailed from the Western Districts and was later the father-in-law of Olympic Gold Medallist Cathy Freeman.

Murrumgunarriman (Twopenny) Toured England with the Australian Aboriginal team in 1868.

Harry Musgrove Was plucked from XXII of Ballarat straight into Australia's Test team after a New Year strike by the leading players. A theatrical promoter for JC Williamson, he was in Ballarat purely for work, when one of his cricket mates from Melbourne told him that the English were in town for a two-day bush international. Would he like to play? 'Are you kidding?' said Harry M. 'Yes, of course I would.' In at number three, he made the century of his life and within days was playing for his country. While he failed in both innings and was never chosen again, he'd had his 15 minutes of fame, in January 1885.

'A Michelle' & other cricket terms

Barbecue: *To run out your batting partner with a poor or injudicious call.*

Beamer: *A head-high full toss.*

Bosie: *An off-break bowled with a leg spinner's action. Named after turn-of-the-century Englishman BJT Bosanquet.*

Bunsen: *A 'Bunsen burner'; rhyming slang for a raging turner [a big-turning pitch].*

Buzzers: *Overthrows.*

Cack-hander: *A leftie. Five of Australia's top six were lefties in the inaugural Test vs Sri Lanka, 1983.*
See Mollydooker.

'A Michelle' & other cricket terms continues overleaf . . .

... 'A Michelle' & other cricket terms continued

Chin music: *Intimidating deliveries delivered fast and at the throat.*

Chinaman: *A left-arm wrist spinner's orthodox delivery spinning back into the right-handers.*

Cow corner: *Deep midwicket, a favourite hitting area.*

Diamond duck: *Run out without facing a ball.*

Devil's number: *87.*

Doodlebug: *A deliberate beamer, aimed straight at the batsman's head.*

Doosra: *A leg-break bowled with an off-spinner's action; a speciality of the Sri Lankan Muthiah Muralidaran.*

Dot ball: *No run.*

Flipper: *One of Shane Warne's favourite variations of the '90s, a faster, sliding ball zeroing in on the stumps.*

Globe: *A duck.*

Golden age of cricket: *The halcyon period from 1897 to 1913, dominated by so many golden greats from Trumper to Ranji.*

Golden duck: *Out first ball without scoring.*

Google: *A right-arm wrist spinner's wrong 'un, bosie or googly.*

Grubber: *A ball that scuttles through low.*

Ferret: *A specialist number 11. Think Bruce Reid.*

Jaffa: *An unplayable delivery.*

… 'A Michelle' & other cricket terms continued

King pair: *Out first ball in each innings.*

LB: *Short for lbw, leg before wicket.*

Mankad: *When a bowler runs out a batsman at the non-striker's end while he is backing up. It is named after the post-war Indian player Vinoo Mankad.*

'A Michelle': *Taking a 'five-for' in an innings, rhyming slang based on the name of actress Michelle Pfeiffer.*

Mollydooker: *A left hander.*

Out of the screws: *Middling a ball; timing it perfectly.*

A pair: *Dismissed without scoring twice in a match.*

Pearler: *See Jaffa.*

Plumb: *A certain lbw.*

Poles: *Wickets.*

Primary: *A first-ball duck by an Australian player, triggering an automatic donation from members of the Primary Club.*

Rabbit: *A late-order batter; numbers nine, 10 and 11; king, queen, jack.*

Red ink: *Not out.*

Salmon: *See Plumb.*

Sweeper: *Outrider.*

Track: *Pitch.*

Wheelhouse: *In the slot.*

Zoota: *Another Warnie favourite.*

MCG HAPPENINGS

DECEMBER 2012

Sri Lanka concedes the Christmas Test, despite losing only seven wickets in its second innings. Its champion Kumar Sangakkara has his hand fractured by Mitchell Johnson and retires hurt, while two tailenders do not bat. Sri Lanka's second innings lasts just 25 overs, the Australians winning by an innings.

DECEMBER 1999

After a summertime thunderstorm forced play to be abandoned early, an MCG streaker enlivens proceedings by aquaplaning across the soggy outfield and jumping the members' fence, evading security guards and, amid wild cheering, avoiding a hefty fine.

DECEMBER 1980

Noted number 11 Jim Higgs gloves a bouncer from NZ's slow-medium bowler Lance Cairns through to wicketkeeper Warren Lees, only for the umpire, Robin Bailhache, to call 'no ball' on grounds of intimidation; Law 42 (8). Higgs then helps Doug Walters complete his 15th Test century in his comeback season, Walters accelerating from 77 to 107.

DECEMBER 1974

Robin Bailhache and Tom Brooks are upstaged when two appropriately dressed 'fake' umpires stroll to the middle, to rousing cheers, to recommence play after a delay for bad light on day two of the Boxing Day Ashes Test. The crowd is fooled into believing the impostors are genuine.

... MCG happenings continued

JANUARY 1971

Thousands of fans protest at the tame finish to the fifth Ashes Test, clanking empty beer cans against the fence in unison. The 'Beer Can Symphony' continues through the post-match interviews. Set 271 in four hours, England crawls to none for 161.

DECEMBER 1967

Graham McKenzie takes six pre-lunch wickets for Australia against India, including a wicket in each of his first five overs.

JANUARY 1955

Frank Tyson sends everyone home early, most with their cut lunches untouched, after he takes six for 16 from 51 balls as England mows through the Australians on the fifth morning of the most momentous post-war Ashes Test of them all. See Jack House

FEBRUARY 1948

In only his second Test and his first in his hometown of Melbourne, Fitzroy teenager Neil Harvey reaches a century with an all-run 'five', in the fifth Australia vs India Test.

FEBRUARY 1929

The MCG hosts the first eight-day Test match which produces 1554 runs and results in a five-wicket victory for Australia, its only win of the summer.

Belinda Clark was the first Aussie, male or female, to make a double century in an ODI.

Clark family archives

Parliamentarian Don Chipp pictured with Gary Cosier, Jim Higgs and John Scholes in Adelaide representing Old Victoria against Old South Australia at the Adelaide Oval in 1986.

Ray Titus

Boy Wonder Michael Clarke signed a six-figure contract with Slazenger before he'd played a Test.

75-year-old Billy Coghlan took five wickets in five balls.
Australian Cricket Society/ *Pavilion* magazine

The celebrated Victor Trumper attended Crown Street Public School in inner Sydney, playing his first match for its second XI as an 11-year-old in 1888.

Arthur Chipperfield was out for 99 on his Ashes debut.

Rising allrounder Alan Davidson was just 20 when he became the first to take a 'ten-for' and make a hundred in the same representative match, at Masterton, NZ, in 1949–50.

Ian Davis, the Boy Wonder of the '70s. He hailed from Nowra, made his first century as a 10-year-old and opened Australia's batting in the 1977 centenary Test.

Bob Cowper with Sir Donald Bradman after his epic 307, still the MCG Test record. Weeks earlier the Don had accused Cowper of not being fit enough and dropped him to 12th man.

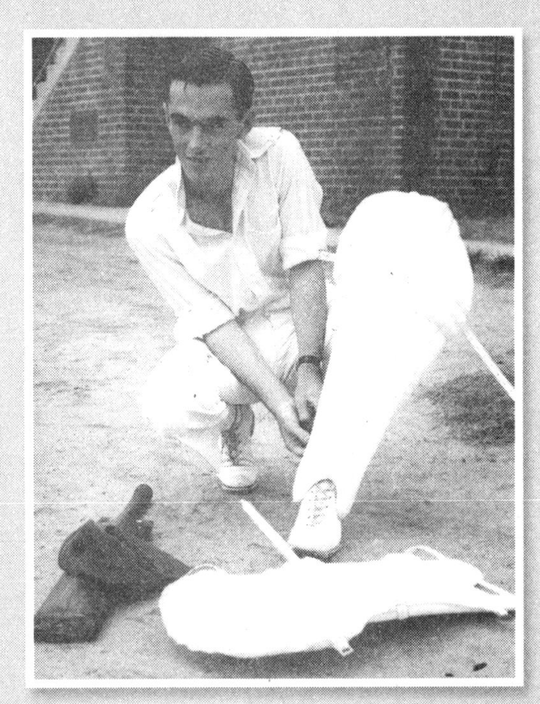

Ian Craig captained Australia at 22.

Cricketer–journalist Jack Fingleton penned Cricket Crisis, *one of the most acclaimed cricket books of all, in 1946.*

Mick Hinman, the boy prodigy from Maitland, took a 'five-for' against Walter Hammond's touring English in 1946–47.

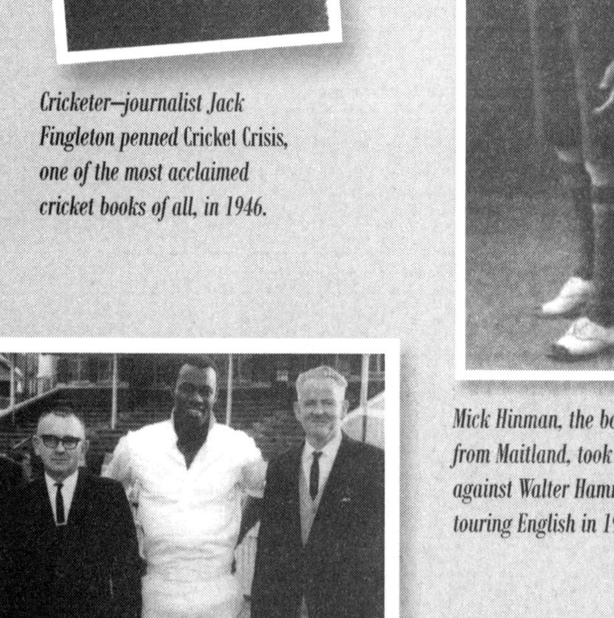

George Wintle (left) and Randwick CC's president Bill Beath with their star import from Barbados, Wes Hall – the most celebrated cricketer in the world in the mid-'60s.

Heads turned when the tanned Charlie McLaughlin walked shirtless into Randwick Oval and asked to have a bowl ...

Late-bloomer Jack Iverson went from Brighton thirds into Test cricket in four years.

Norman O'Neill had a wicked sense of humor.

Frank O'Keeffe was on the verge of Test cricket when he contracted peritonitis and died young.

White-ball specialist Peter Morelli, the heaviest opening batsman in Australasia.

Alf Wilson/*Bradmans of the Bush*

Queensland country legend Michael Sippel from Ipswich has an extraordinary all-round record.

The Queensland Times

The 'Bradman' of women's cricket, Betty Wilson was the first to make a century and take 10 wickets in a Test match.

Nagel to North

Lisle & Vernon Nagel Identical 198 centimetre (six foot six) fast-bowling twins from Brighton, Victoria. Lisle parted his blond hair down the middle and Vern parted his to the right. On one country trip to Bendigo at Easter 1935, Vern went off to play some tennis and when he hadn't reappeared at the fall of the ninth wicket, Lisle went out and batted for him. Both played for Victoria. Lisle also had one Bodyline Test.

Dirk Nannes Represented The Netherlands at Lord's before first appearing for Australia at a mature age of 33, at white-ball level, in the winter of 2009.

Brendan Nash A 'white' West Indian, he played all his initial first-class cricket in Queensland, once batting 88 minutes without scoring, before representing the West Indies in 21 Tests. His father was born in Jamaica and his mother in England. Nash played his formative cricket at Nudgee (now St Joseph's Nudgee) College in Brisbane.

Laurie Nash A brash and bumper-happy paceman, he was selected purely from club ranks for his two Tests in the '30s, bypassing the Sheffield Shield.

Nervous Nineties No Australian Ashes batsman has been dismissed more often in the 90s than Clem Hill. After his 99 (Melbourne, 1901–02), he followed with innings of 98 and 97 in the very next Test in Adelaide.

New Italy CC Formed at Coraki, northern NSW, in 1898. At the inaugural meeting, approval was given for the purchase of a bat (at 12 shillings and sixpence) and a ball (at five shillings and sixpence).

The initial members were: G Nardi, A Spinaze, G Spinaze, G Bazzo, F Roder, J Rosolen (playing secretary), L Rosolen, P Morandini, D Antoniolli, N Capelin, N Pezzuti, G Picco and B Battistuzzi.

Bill Newton The tall, lean and handsome St Kilda fast bowler was beheaded on the beach at Salamaua, New Guinea, having been captured when his plane was forced down by enemy fire in early 1943. His low-level assaults in 'Boston' bombers had seen him make 52 enemy raids in a 10-month period from May 1942. Newton was to be awarded a posthumous Victoria Cross for his wartime bravery.

His solitary representative cricket game, in 1939, was with the Victorian Colts (seconds) at the MCG, a game in which he took the wicket of a 16-year-old budding champion, Arthur Morris.

The 'next Bradman' A tag bestowed on several rising champions by the influential, one-eyed Sydney press in the '50s, most notably Ian Craig and Norman O'Neill.

John Nichols Took five catches at first slip, a Geelong CA single-innings record: North Geelong vs St Josephs, 1973–74. Four came from the bowling of finger spinner Rod Walsh.

Angelo Nicosia The first Italian to umpire a Test match: Australian Women vs English Women, Queen Elizabeth Oval, Bendigo, January 1985.

Jack (Slinger) Nitschke Played two early 1930s Tests for Australia against South Africa. Later enjoyed prolonged success as a breeder of quality racehorses including Dayana, winner of the 1972 VRC Derby and the 1973 Perth Cup.

Geff Noblet The misspelling of his given name was a mistake made on his birth certificate.

Ashley Noffke One of just three to take 50 wickets and make 500 runs for his state, Queensland, in a first-class season, 2007–08. The others were George Giffen (South Australia) and Greg Matthews (NSW).

Marcus North Once took a 'six-for' at Lord's but is better known for his five Test centuries.

O'Brien to Oxford

Leo O'Brien The old Bodyliner mixed batting with boxing, having 30 fights including a shot at the Victorian lightweight title, the only bout he ever lost.

As Australia's 12th man in the Adelaide Bodyline Test in 1933, he told teammates of captain Bill Woodfull's terse conversation with England's esteemed team manager, the soon-to-be-knighted Plum Warner. The story was 'leaked' by one of the players – Jack Fingleton blamed Don Bradman – and the subsequent newspaper headlines and set of administrative cables from London back to Sydney almost stopped the tour.

Simon O'Donnell His enormous straight six landed in the second tier of the MCG's Shane Warne Stand, then known as the Great Southern Stand. 'It's big, isn't it?' said the bowler, NSW's Greg Matthews, refusing to look.

Kevin O'Dowd Worked for 12,000 hours on the only edition of the *Geelong Cricketers Almanac*, published in 1999. As part of his Bradman-like research, he scanned 24,000 daily editions of the *Geelong Advertiser*.

O'Grady's Ridge XI Its home ground was an oddly shaped paddock belonging to Gippsland farmer Mr Vic Martin. So close was the southern boundary that, if hit, two rather than four runs would be recorded.

Jack O'Hagan Wrote and performed the still-popular tribute song, 'Our Don Bradman' in 1930.

Frank O'Keeffe Twin centuries against the likes of Gregory, McDonald and Mailey for The Rest vs Australia (Sydney, February 1922) would have guaranteed him a

place in the Test team, but there was a break of almost three years between Tests. He missed his chance and died young, at 27, from peritonitis. Is credited with having invented the practice of fielders moving in with the bowler. Previously they had been totally still.

'Old Fashioned Locket' & 'Our Bungalow of Dreams' Piano solos recorded by Don Bradman for Columbia Records in the early 1930s.

David Oman Lismore's 'Don Bradman', he made a club record 10,857 runs over four decades from 1964.

One hundred and five runs in a row John Pellew (cousin of Testman 'Nip'): Grange vs Woodville, Adelaide, January 1913.

Norman O'Neill Batting for the first time for a Combined XI against the unnerving raw pace of West Indian Wes Hall, Normie was asked where he'd like the sightscreen. 'About halfway down the pitch, between Wes and I,' he said, at the WACA Ground in 1960.

Charlie Onus Shared in consecutive opening stands of 444 and 335 three days apart in Maitland club cricket: Albion, NSW, November 1901.

Oops Asked to predict the likely outcome of the 1978–79 Ashes series, Australia's first-time captain Graham Yallop said, 'Australia six–nil.' His team lost five Tests and won only one.

Bill O'Reilly Having taken eight for 33 in his final Test, aged 40, the legendary Tiger wearily took off his much-worn ankle-high cricket boots and threw them out of the Basin Reserve's dressing room window. He'd played his last major match: Wellington, NZ, March 1946. *See* Wingello Oval

Bill Orme Made five hundreds in five consecutive games with South Wagga in the late '50s. Twice captained Southern Riverina XIs against touring English teams.

Gus Oxenham Toombul's Oxenham Park is named in his honour, for all his fine administrative work helping to propel Queensland into Sheffield Shield ranks in the 1920s. His son, Ron, represented Australia. Another son, Lionel, played with Queensland.

Oxford's incredible comeback Having made just 93 in the 1979–80 Casino CA Grand Final and seen the opposition, Commonwealth Magpies, reach five for 92 in reply, Oxford's Neville Haywood and Bob Leitch took the final five wickets for 0 to ensure the premiership, by one run.

Paine to Puddin'

Tim Paine Resigned the Australian captaincy in extraordinary circumstances in 2021 after a texting scandal involving himself, his brother-in-law, fellow cricketer Shannon Tubb and a former employee of Cricket Tasmania.

Una Paisley On debut, she became the first Australian woman to make a Test century: Australia vs NZ, Basin Reserve, Wellington, March 1948. The leading women's club cricketer annually in Melbourne receives the Una Paisley Medal.

Joey Palmer The first Australian to score 1000 runs and take 100 wickets on an Ashes tour in 1886.

Dr Roy Park Was bowled by the only delivery he faced in Tests: Melbourne 1920. He'd been up all night attending a difficult birth.

Years later, Dr Park said: 'The [generous] reception I received may have subconsciously subtracted from that intense concentration so essential to [good] batting.

'It was not cricket "nerves". I had no reason to be on edge. I had been making good scores against all comers. It was just one of those things.

'My friends took the failure more to heart then me. Cricket is such a game. Centuries and ducks get mixed up in most cricketers' careers.'

Frank Parry Kim Hughes's coach. He was forever telling the teenager that he'd not only play for Australia but he'd also be captain. He was right on both counts.

See Brisbane Test happenings

P

Len Pascoe Having lingered too long, once again, at an after-match function, Lenny returned home late to wife Elaine, who proceeded to rip to shreds the scrapbook she had kept on him for years.

Was born Len Durtanovich.

Darren Pattinson Melbourne-raised, he played one Test for England midway through a cricketing holiday in the UK, in 2008.

Tom Patton The first 'bushie' to score a quadruple century (408 for Buffalo River vs Whorouly, Gapstead 1913–14), he shared a mega-stand of 641 for the third wicket with Norman Rippon (321). 'We fancy it must be some sort of record,' said the local writer in the *Myrtleford Mail and Whorouly Witness*.

Patton's great score was later equalled by Griffith CYMS's Keith Savage, in a semifinal in 1950–51. Just 158 centimetres tall (five foot two), Savage hit 66 fours and not even one six. Around this time Savage and his opening partner Arthur Clifton Jnr (Alan Davidson's uncle) amassed three triple-century stands in three consecutive matches.

Mick Pawley A legend of Sydney grade cricket whose career spanned 22 years. In 1973–74 he took 62 wickets at under 10 for Manly–Warringah and made 263 runs at 30.

Allan Pearson Scored 212 before lunch, Fernleigh vs Eureka, Clunes and District, late 1930s.

Margaret Peden Captained the first Australian women's team to tour England in 1937.

Nip Pellew Unbeaten in 10 Tests as a player, he later coached with flair and authority, his last year as South Australia's head coach coming at the age of 77.

Pentridge Prison Was the venue for the launch of Merv Hughes's best-selling book *My Life and Other Funny Stories* (1990).

Cec Pepper The best cricketer never to play for Australia and the highest paid professional in the world immediately after World War II, his big-hitting exploits included a hit of 165 yards (151 metres) at Woodward Park in Parkes, NSW, in 1935–36. From the southern end, the ball steepled clear of the pickets, the parked cars, the tennis courts and finished in Victoria Street, outside the Showground gates. Once, in England, he hit a ball into Trafalgar Square ... Scarborough, not London!

Clinton Perren The durable, seasoned Queenslander once scored 181 in a 50-over match in the Central Lancashire League in the early 2000s.

Ellyse Perry First represented Australia at 16, before she'd even played for New South Wales. Possessor of intoxicating talent, she scored a famous goal for the Matildas [Australia's soccer team] against Sweden during the 2011 FIFA Women's World Cup in Germany. A decade later she was named the ICC's Cricketer of the Decade and in 2022 batted in the top six for Australia in its undefeated World Cup title in NZ.

Peter Who? Peter Taylor, the seasoned off-spinner selected for his first Ashes Test, despite having played only one Sheffield Shield game all summer. Some thought the selectors had named the wrong Taylor: 30-year-old Peter instead of 22-year-old Mark. With eight wickets and 53 runs for the game, he was man of the match in Sydney, January 1987.

Phantom Bill Lawry's nickname, bestowed by his teammate Dick Maddocks after Lawry packed a bundle of his favourite Phantom comics with him on his first interstate tour, by train, to Adelaide in 1956.

Jim Phillips No-balled famed Australian speedster Ernie Jones twice in the opening weeks of the 1897–98 Ashes summer, the first in Adelaide and the second during the New Year Test match in Melbourne. Both matches involved AE Stoddart's touring English team. Jones was never no-balled anywhere again.

Scotty Phillips The first Mornington Peninsula A grader to take a 'ten-for'. Actually it was 13 as, in the same Sorrento innings, he bowled three others with no balls! It took him 16 overs to secure his first wicket. His final figures were 10 for 44 from 26 overs: Long Island vs Sorrento, Sorrento Oval, November 1992.

Wayne Phillips So assured was the South Australian batsman–wicketkeeper against the famed West Indians in the 1984 Bridgetown Test that his teammates dubbed him Spaceman. His 120 from number eight was scored in a hurry against three of the finest fast bowlers of any generation: Malcolm Marshall, Joel Garner and Michael Holding.

Peter Philpott The ex-Test leg spinner played Clarrie Grimmett in the seven-part mini-series *Bodyline*, released in 1984. *See also* Gary Sweet

Joe Plant Taught a young Neil Harvey how to dance down the wicket at Fitzroy CC's nets at Brunswick Street, early 1940s.

Jack Pollard His CV of 97 sporting books either written, edited or published is unequalled. The majority were on cricket and included his iconic anthology *Six and Out*, first released in 1964. The Australian Cricket Society's annual Literary Award is named in Jack's honour.

Luke Pomersbach His only Australian appearance came at the eleventh hour in hometown Perth when Brad Hodge was a late withdrawal from a Twenty20 international. Using borrowed gear, including Hodge's shirt with DODGEBALL on the back, he made 15: WACA Ground, 2007–08.

Bill Ponsford A champion who was colourblind, he broke Archie MacLaren's solo record when he made 429 for Victoria against Tasmania (MCG, 1923). The Englishman complained to the Marylebone Cricket Club and *Wisden* that his record (of 424 in 1895) should remain, as he alleged that the two Australian teams were sub first-class standard. He even threatened *Wisden* editor Sydney Pardon with MCC censure should he not back down. Four years later, 'Ponny', a run-making Colossus, scored 437 in a Sheffield Shield match and became the first person to score 1000 first-class runs before the end of December.

Ricky Ponting Signed his first bat contract with Kookaburra at 13, having made five centuries in a week-long high school carnival in Launceston, Tasmania. The Ponting Foundation, run by Ricky and his wife Rianna, has raised millions for families with cancer sufferers.

Hunter Poon The first player of Chinese descent to play first-class cricket: Melbourne, December 1923.

Ron Porter Became an instant hero of all Bendigo when he hit back-to-back fours from the bowling of Bodyliner Harold Larwood on his way to a top score of 55 in a two-day friendly leading into the infamous Adelaide Test match in January 1933. A Porter six, from the bowling of George Geary, landed in the middle row of the Upper Reserve's magnificent Federation grandstand.

Jack Potter The most often wedded of all Aussie internationals, he married four times and still answers to the sobriquet Willie. (South Africa's Hugh Tayfield and England's Bill Edrich married five times each; one of the guests at Edrich's last wedding, fellow Test cricketer John Warr, was taking his seat when an usher approached: 'Groom's side or bride's?' 'Season ticket,' replied Warr.)

Potter was three times Australia's 12th man and brilliantly ran out South Africa's Eddie Barlow during a brief stint as a substitute in Melbourne in January 1964.

He was denied a Test opportunity after the Ashes tour in 1964, having suffered a fractured skull in an exhibition match between Tests on a matting wicket at The Hague.

John Power Prahran's opening bowler of the 1950s regularly used his false teeth as a marker at the top of his run-up.

Joe Previtera The Channel 9 cameraman whose throwaway line, 'Can't bowl, can't throw' – accidentally broadcast via an effects microphone – incensed Scott Muller, who claimed his Aussie teammate Shane Warne had said it: Hobart, 1999–2000.

Karen Price On her way to Australian representation, she played seven seasons of A and B grade men's cricket with Normanhurst, taking 200-plus wickets in the Hornsby, Ku-ring-gai and Hills District CA, 1970s.

Terry Prindiville First selected for Western Australia at the age of 26, he looked years older because of his silver–grey hair.

Puddin' Bill Ponsford's nickname.

Quick to Quinsee

Q

Ian Quick Don Bradman's penchant for having a left-arm finger spinner in every Ashes touring party saw Quick, from Geelong, promoted after his 32 wickets in the 1960–61 Australian season. He played almost every county game, but none of the Tests, and soon drifted out of even Sheffield Shield ranks.

Laurie Quinlan Made the fastest century in Australian minor cricket: 100 not out in 18 minutes from 4.41 p.m. to 4.59 p.m. one memorable Cairns Saturday for Trinity vs Mercantile, 1909–10. His score sequence was 26241162364436266414424646 1.
See Eighteen-minute hundreds

John Quinn The Kyabram-based truckie regularly played two games with two different teams in two different Associations each Saturday during the '60s and '70s. He was always apologetic for arriving late, or leaving early.

Jack Quinsee Was square leg umpiring this day at Welshpool when a ball was pulled in his direction. Throwing himself headlong at the ball, he took it in one hand before realising who he was and what he was doing and quickly released it.

'Sorry fellas,' he said. 'Sheer habit.'

QUIPS

Shane Warne loved emojis and worked with cartoonist Paul Harvey on a range of fun ones, sending up his hair, love of fast food, cars and women.

'He was fun to work with and was up for almost anything,' said Harvey. 'Among the few designs we changed was the emoji of Warnie in a spa with two Indian girls. He reckoned this might be seen as culturally insensitive.

'But,' he said to me, 'you can put two blondes in there, though ... that's fine.'

...

When South Africa's Daryll Cullinan returned to the Melbourne Cricket Ground in 1997 he brushed past his nemesis Shane Warne. 'I've been waiting three years for another chance to get you,' said Warne. 'Looks like you spent it eating,' said Cullinan.

Cullinan averaged 44 in Tests but only 12 against Australia.

...

Few were as provocative as Pakistan's Javed Miandad, who turned heads everywhere he played. Looking to antagonise Australia's Merv Hughes, Javed said, 'You're (just) a bus conductor Hughes ... a bus conductor.'

Minutes later Hughes dismissed Javed and as he turned for the Adelaide members, big Merv extended his follow through and stretching out both hands he smiled broadly at Javed and said, 'Tickets please!'

...

The West Indian express Patrick Patterson was introduced to Sir Donald Bradman in Adelaide in 1988. 'Wow,' he said. 'You're only a little bloke ... I would have knocked your head off.'

... Quips continued

'You'd need to improve,' said the Don. 'You can't even get Merv Hughes out.' (Earlier that day Merv had made a Test-high 72 not out.)

'Well how many do you think you'd average against me?'

'Oh,' said the Don. '55 ... maybe 56.'

'Only 56?'

'Well I am 80, you know.'

...

Steve Waugh was taking an eternity marking his guard, settling himself before facing his first ball in a Sheffield Shield match. 'For Christ's sake, mate. It's not a fuckin' Test match!' called Jamie Siddons from slip.

'Of course it's not,' said Waugh. 'You're here'.

...

Alan Mullally was 18 and barely shaving when he made his first-class debut in the 1987–88 Sheffield Shield final in Perth. Tough-as-teak icon Allan Border approached. Looking him up and down, he said, 'Not at school today, sonny?'

Mullally later played Test cricket, for England.

...

At the height of a keenly fought World Series one-dayer in Sydney in the late '80s, Australia's wicketkeeper Ian Healy eyed Sri Lanka's rotund captain Arjuna Ranatunga and said, 'You can't get a runner because you're fat.'

Earlier in the tour, Healy suggested the Aussies put a hot dog outside the crease as a lure to Ranatunga to use his feet more.

'It won't work,' said Ranatunga. 'Boony will get there first.'

QUOTES

'Warnie is probably the greatest cricketer who has ever been.' – RICKY PONTING

———

'I'd rather watch ripe bananas brown than watch Justin Langer bat.' – KERRY O'KEEFFE

———

'His idea of a short single is a tap to bat pad.' – IAN CHAPPELL on Michael Bevan.

———

'I just shuffle up and go "wang".' – JEFF THOMSON

———

'There are 500,000 other cricketers in Australia who'd love to play.' – ultra-conservative administrator ALAN BARNES refusing to empathise with the players over their wage demands in the early 1970s.

———

'Well bowled, bird brain.' – Australia's touring captain BILL LAWRY to Ashley Mallett in South Africa, 1970.

———

'People look at you as though you have two heads and six fingers. They reckon I bowl six different balls. That's hogwash.' – JOHN GLEESON

———

'Australia's cricket captains have been plumbers, graziers, dentists, whisky agents, crime reporters, letter sorters, boot-sellers, handicappers, shopkeepers and postmen.' – CHRISTIAN RYAN

... Quotes continued

'I saw much better batsmen than I was; lots of them. They just kept getting out.' – SIR DONALD BRADMAN

— — —

'Johnno [Ian Johnson] and Nugget [Keith Miller] weren't friends. Yet one was captain and the other was vice-captain.' – COLIN McDONALD.

— — —

'There will never be a player like him again.' – GIDEON HAIGH on Jack Iverson.

— — —

'Forget all the games I'm said to have saved; just once I'd have liked to have won a game for Australia.' – ALLAN BORDER.

— — —

'Sir Donald Bradman was the greatest of all batsmen I have watched [and] the most valuable and devastating batsman any Test team ever owned.' – Bodyline umpire GEORGE HELE

— — —

'How fortunate Australia is in the matter of cricket stars. Just as the bright sun of Bradman's cricket glory sets, there is a new sun rising in the east in the person of a young Neil Harvey, a mere boy, who in the tradition of the other youthful Australian players like McCabe, Jackson and Brown of recent memory, saw the chance to leap to cricket fame and never hesitated a moment in the quest.' – ANDY FLANAGAN

— — —

'The ball seemed to melt into his gloves.' – LINDSAY HASSETT, enthusing at the glovesmanship of fellow Bradman Invincible Don Tallon.

R

Rae to Ryan

Dawn Rae Shared a record 478-run opening stand with Jan Wilkinson for inner-city Melbourne's Olympic CC, 1974–75. Her personal best score of 249 came the following summer.

Vernon Ransford The Golden Age left-hander beat the young Don Bradman for the role of Melbourne Cricket Club secretary in 1938. At the time, Ransford was 53 and Bradman 29.

Rawling family Four family members, father Doug and his three sons David, Peter and John, all scored centuries in the same Maitland club season, 1974–75.

Ian Redpath The pencil-thin opener would stuff his breast pocket and creams with handkerchiefs to provide extra padding against short-pitched bowling. Ran an antiques business in Geelong for years.

Ron Reed When a 20-year-old Pommy named Ian Botham briefly joined our Melbourne midweek team The Plastic XI in 1977, he was immediately shuffled to first-change duties by Reed, the captain and opening bowler (known as The Hound and loved for his twinkletoed, short-stepped approach to the wicket, *à la* cartoon favourite, Fred Flintstone).

That winter Botham took two 'five-fors' in his maiden two Ashes Tests for England. Only then did we concede that maybe The Hound was wrong.

Edward Reedman Was rising 73, the oldest A grade cricketer in Australia, when he filled in for his son Dinny's team, North Adelaide, at Unley Oval in

1903–04. Not worrying about pads, he survived four overs, helping his son add 22 important runs in a narrow victory.

Bruce Reid With one to tie and two to win a World Series 50-over white-ball game at Bellerive, Australia's perennial number 11 missed five of the six final balls from New Zealand's Chris Pringle and was run out from the last, giving NZ a memorable one-run win in 1990. 'It was one of the great overs,' said the respected NZ writer and ex-selector Don Neely.

Reid averaged 4.65 in Tests and 7.85 in all first-class matches. 'He was the world's worst (batsman),' Pringle was to say later.

Paul Reiffel Loves to remind everyone of the time he and Glenn McGrath bowled England out for 77 at Lord's in 1997. 'We basically bowled unchanged,' he says. 'I took two wickets and Glenn grabbed the rest!'

Dave Renneberg Dismissed the world's number one batsman, South Africa's Graeme Pollock, in his first over of his debut Test at Johannesburg in 1966–67. Batted 13 times in Tests without once making double figures.

Arthur Richardson Scored a century and took 10 wickets in an innings in the same game at Mintaro Oval, Clare, South Australia, in 1913. He learnt to play on the family's slate wicket in a back paddock at Sevenhill.

Was a fortnight short of his 38th birthday when he made his one and only Test century against England at Headingley in 1926.

Doug Ring The old Bradman Invincible was the long-time face of cricket on Channel Seven's Sunday lunchtime institution, *World of Sport*. His conversation and genial interviews were spiced by the occasional off-mark forecast, including the time, in 1967, when he predicted Victoria's star-studded batting line-up could break the world record in its opening match against Western Australia in Perth. With eight Test players in its XI, the Vics were bowled out for 152, 955 runs short. Ian Brayshaw took 10 for 44.

Steve Rixon The straight-talking, no-nonsense country boy from Albury so upset Viv Richards during the New Year Test in Sydney, 1985, that the West Indian, dressed in nothing but a towel, marched through the members' bar only to be met at the door by a band of astonished Aussie cricket writers. Rixon had earlier suggested that, as good as Viv was, he couldn't bat *and* umpire the game.

Ray Robinson Co-inventor of the term 'Bodyline' and Australia's foremost post-war cricket writer, his acclaimed first book *Between Wickets* (1946) went into an unprecedented seven editions.

Sugar Ray's colourful pieces remained a feature in my magazine *Cricketer* four decades later when he was well into his 70s. Writing of the epic Kline–Mackay match-saving partnership in Adelaide in 1960–61, Robinson dubbed it 'the longest last stand since Custer's'. It was his last published essay in the October 1982 edition.

Rayford Robinson Don Bradman once said of him, 'If you ever saw Ray Robinson make a hundred, you'd forget about me.' Yet the Boy Wonder from the Hunter region was to average only 31 in representative ranks and make just two and three in his only Test match, in Brisbane in 1936. Led a tragic later life.

Richie Robinson The season of his life with Victoria in 1976–77 included four centuries in consecutive matches, but he was a flop as Australia's opener in the Jubilee Test series that immediately followed. 'Given a second chance, I would have liked to have played like an Adam Gilchrist and really gone after the bowling from the start,' he said.

Dr Harry Rock Boasts a higher Sheffield Shield batting average than even Don Bradman: 112 from his four matches for NSW in the 1920s. His grip was so high on the handle and he stood so upright that bowlers opposing him for the first time thought he wasn't ready to face up. He'd badly injured his knees in World War I and had to adopt an entirely new stance.

His father Claude had been a Launceston stalwart, captained his state and scored Tasmania's first first-class century, against Victoria, in 1889.

Rocket-arms Eldine Baptiste (Geelong City & West Indies), Ernie Bromley (St Kilda & Australia), Bill Ellison (Randwick), Murray Hill (Beaumaris), Rhys McConachy (Lismore), Bill Moule (Victoria & Australia), Norman O'Neill (NSW & Australia), Paul Sheahan (Victoria & Australia), Stan Stephens (Prahran & Victoria).

Luke Ronchi The only cricketer to represent both Australia and New Zealand. Once made a 22-ball half-century for Australia at St Kitts. Also has a 54-ball Sheffield Shield century in his CV. The first of his four Tests for NZ was against England at Leeds in 2015. He made 88 and 31 in a hurry and took four catches in a rousing victory.

Gordon Rorke On his MCG debut, the NSW express conceded 12 runs from his first four balls: three lots of four byes in Melbourne, December 1957. Victoria's opener Allen Aylett had never faced anyone as quick ... or as wayward.

John Rutherford Western Australia's first Test representative from Bruce Rock, near Merredin. A century in a Test trial in Sydney on the eve of the 1956 Ashes tour selection clinched his place as reserve opener. Talking of the young mathematics teacher's origins, one eastern states feature writer said Rutherford hailed from a small town, 170 miles west of Perth – placing him somewhere in the Indian Ocean!

Bill Ryan After senior partner Fred Zeuschner scored four runs from the opening over in a Gippsland matting match, Ryan made the next 99 himself, before being run out going for his 100th run: Leongatha vs Stony Creek–Mirboo North, 1939. While overshadowed this day, Zeuschner was to become the finest batsman in Gippsland in the immediate post-war years.

Sabburg to Symes

Chris Sabburg The red-headed Saturdays-only player substituted for Ryan Harris in a hometown Ashes Test and caught England's Kevin Pietersen at deep fine leg, having been on the field for just two balls: Brisbane 2013.

John Savigny The first Northern Tasmanian CA batsman to make 1000 runs in a season, 1902.

Karl Schneider A child prodigy from Xavier College, just 157 centimetres (five foot one) and 55 kilograms (eight stone nine), he died young at 23, his talent unfulfilled; a tour of New Zealand in the late 1920s with an Australian B team his only representative cricket. *See* Xavier College

Eliza (Granny) Scholz The midwife who delivered baby Donald George Bradman at 89 Adams Street, Cootamundra, NSW, on 27 August 1908. 'Don was a bonny baby and a sturdy little chap,' she said years later.

Jeff Scotland Made a matchwinning 76 not out from 29 balls: Australian Cricket Society Over 60s vs Benalla, Kyabram, March 2022. Fifty-two of his runs came in two overs.

Jack Scott The first to bowl Bodyline, seven years before Larwood and co. Scott's arc of close-catching fielders stretched from the wicketkeeper to square leg. Victoria's captain Edgar Mayne was considerably disconcerted by the bumper barrage. Scott's first over lasted 13 balls, umpire Wally French no-balling him five times for 'dragging': NSW vs Victoria, Sydney, January 1925.

S

Arnold Seitz Dux at Scotch College, a Rhodes Scholar, Oxford 'blue' and Victorian Director of Education, he was also a Victorian cricket captain (1912–13) and president of the Victorian Cricket Association from 1947–62.

Des Selby Glenelg's wicketkeeper at the height of chinaman bowler David Sincock's club career, he'd urge opposing batsmen unable to pick the direction of Sincock's prodigious, unpredictable spin 'to get down the wicket and hit it before it can turn'. His celebrations when they were stumped were always full-on.

Malcolm Semple Took a 'ten-for' all bowled: St David's Glenhuntly Under 14s vs St Andrew's Gardiner Under 14s, Glenhuntly, January 1970. His final figures were 8.2–2–16–10.

James Sharp Amassed an Australian interschool record 506 not out for Melbourne Grammar against Geelong College in 1914–15. He never made another hundred.

Bill Sheahan The first to umpire 400 First XI matches in Premier League cricket ranks in Melbourne.

Paul Sheahan Once batted 52 minutes and faced 44 balls for 0 not out to help save an Ashes Test at Lord's, in 1968. The boy wonder from Geelong College – scorer of 223 at the age of 17 – was known for his matinee-idol looks, handsome elegance at the crease, magnificent throwing arm and premature exit from the international game at just 27.

Barry Shepherd So sure was Richie Benaud that Shepherd, West Australia's captain and finest batsman, would be chosen for the 1964 Ashes tour that he presented him with his prized leather cricket bag, with the embossing 'R. BENAUD'. Shepherd missed selection but kept the bag.

Dave Sherwood Was Australia's official scorer on six consecutive Ashes tours from 1964. Scored for Randwick at first-grade level for 52 years.

Ted Sherwood Claimed eight for 50 bowling underarm for Balmain against a Dungog representative XI, Easter 1929.

Essie & Fernie Shevill The first sisters to represent Australia in a Test; Australia vs England, Brisbane Exhibition Ground, December 1934. Fernie played under her married name, Blade. A third sister, Irene Shevill, joined Essie in the team for the second and third Tests.

Shorts The Victorian one-day team wore short pants for one Mercantile Mutual Cup season in 1994–95.

Bob Simpson His surprising comeback, aged 41, after 10 years away from the international game, saw him make 539 runs, average 53 with two centuries against the touring Indians in 1977–78. The Indians were stunned by Simpson's sparkling footwork and composure.

Mathew Sinclair Scored two double centuries in his first dozen Tests with New Zealand, having moved, aged five, from his birthplace at Katherine in the Northern Territory.

Ron Sinclair Maryborough's Mr Cricket, his 900-page local cricket history was typed with one finger after he became crippled with acute arthritis. It took him two and a half years to research and write in the 1980s.

David Sincock Invited to the Adelaide nets by the touring West Indians, the unknown teen spinner stunned the tourists by bowling four of their best players: captain Frank Worrell, Garry Sobers, Rohan Kanhai and Conrad Hunte. Within a week, he was playing for South Australia.

Was known to all as Evil, short for 'evil dick'. His brother, Peter, also a cricketer, was Evil Junior.

Jack Sing Captain of the Geelong CA's Team of the Century – announced in 1997 – his aggregate of 10,251 runs (average 50) and 30 centuries are both Geelong club cricket records. Five of his tons came in 1948–49, four in a row. He played in a near-record eight First XI premierships. He always cherished a half-century he made from number six for a Victorian Country XI against Freddie Brown's English tourists at Geelong late in the summer of 1950–51.

Michael Sippel The legend of the Lockyer Valley, his CV at Ipswich includes 10,000-plus runs and 500-plus wickets, all in the first division. Among two dozen centuries is a high of 261 and best bowling nine for 28. Played just once for Queensland, a one-dayer in 2002. Sells vegetable seeds for a living.

Stan Sismey Responsible for a remarkable 19 dismissals in one match (10 caught and nine stumped): Western Suburbs vs Marrickville, 1939–40. Later kept wickets in the 1945 Victory tests.

Les Sleeman The Nathalia, Victoria, swing king once knocked a bail 70 yards (65 metres) behind the wicket in the early 1900s. Around the same time he took a hat-trick, all bowled, all middle stump.

Graeme Smith A long-time scourge of Canberra club batsmen, Smith was included in the Prime Minister's XI for the biggest game of his life, under the captaincy of Don Bradman at Manuka Oval, Canberra, in 1962–63.

'What would you like Graeme?' asked the Don.

'Mid-on and mid-off right back,' said Smith.

'It's good to encourage them to hit. Let's play them deeper, but not all the way back.'

Each of Smith's first six balls were hit for four by England's David Sheppard before his seventh ballooned to cover. Smith's three for 61 came from eight overs.

In his last 'international', the Don, 54, made four.

Warren Smith Michael Slater's long-time coach from his primary school days at Mount Austin in Wagga, NSW.

Smokers vs Non-smokers A four-day representative game at the East Melbourne CC ground in Jolimont, Melbourne, March 1887. Fielding first, the Smokers entered the arena 'each blowing a cloud from a cigar of colonial manufacture'. The Non-smokers won on the first innings 803 to 356.

Charles Somerville The red-headed boy on whom Jimmy Bancks modelled the cricket-loving comic strip character Ginger Meggs.

Diane Spark Bush cricket's ultimate scorer, the start of season 2022–23 marked her 58th consecutive year of scoring with French Island on Western Port Bay. 'I had to wait 40 years for my first premiership,' she said.

Di also organises the most luscious matchday afternoon teas, her Windsor-style sandwiches, scones and jelly slices ensuring a full house on the ferry trip every second Saturday from Stony Point.

Her father, wicketkeeper–batsman Bob Thompson, was for years the patriarch of the family's cricketing XI. At one stage, six Thompson brothers and their sons made up 10 of the team. One of the boys had a sleeping disorder and occasionally would nod off while standing at mid-off.

Fred Spofforth Australia's most celebrated early bowler and first cricket hero, Spofforth was also the first number 11 to score a Test half-century, in Melbourne, March 1885. He loved the big occasion.

Keith Stackpole Jnr As part of his night-time sleep routine, he shuts his eyes and visualises each of his 15 Test wickets from Colin Cowdrey (1966) through to Roy Fredericks (1973).

Jim Steel Hit eight jet-propelled sixes in eight balls at Queen Elizabeth Oval, Bendigo, in 1984–85. One sailed over the historic grandstand, two others into the curator's cottage and the fourth and mightiest was caught by the wicketkeeper ... on an adjoining ground! His 82 came from 23 balls. His last 10 scoring shots were all sixes. Gisborne's John McCallum conceded 36 from one over.

Gavin Stevens Contracted hepatitis on Australia's tour of Pakistan and India in 1959–60 and never played again. His career-best score was 259 not out.

Dick Stockdale Took five for 0 in one over, without a hat-trick, in a between-the-wars Leongatha & District Grand Final: Koonwarra vs Koorooman, Victoria, 1933.

Anthony Stuart Took a hat-trick in the last of his three ODIs for Australia, in Melbourne, 1996–97.

Jim Sullivan Few spanned the generations quite like the durable Sydneysider, who was coached as a junior by Alick Bannerman, opposed MA (Monty) Noble and Arthur Mailey at the start of his career and Tiger O'Reilly and Ray Lindwall at the end of it.

Sunday cricket Was implemented from 1967–68, everywhere but in the 'city of churches', Adelaide.

Gary Sweet Played Don Bradman in the popular Kennedy–Miller TV miniseries *Bodyline*, released in 1984.

Gavin Symes Balnarring's champion runmaker was about to take his guard against Flinders before realising he'd forgotten his bat: Mornington Peninsula, 1980s.

SCG HAPPENINGS

JANUARY 2017

In Sydney's New Year Test match, fast bowler Jackson Bird takes four catches as a substitute fieldsman, two in Pakistan's first innings and two in their second.

JANUARY 2006

Known for carrying more gear in his bag than any of his contemporaries, Mr Cricket, Mike Hussey, takes to the field in a pair of white heavily studded footy boots after heavy rains make the SCG outfield wet and soggy.

NOVEMBER 1979

Surely there has never been a more defensive field. But at the time, it was within the rules. With the West Indies advancing rapidly in a World Series one-dayer, Mike Brearley insists on every fielder, including wicketkeeper David Bairstow, being on the fence during the deciding over, a key moment as England protects a winning score.

FEBRUARY 1969

Subject of a 'Mankad' dismissal earlier in the series for backing up too far, Ian Redpath is twice caught out of his crease again, at 18 and 64, but this time, neither bowler Wes Hall nor Charlie Griffith effects the run out. 'Don't do that again, maan,' says Griffith in mid-innings. A reprieved Redpath reaches his first Test century in his 28th appearance.

... SCG happenings continued

JANUARY 1951

A fortnight after decimating England in the New Year Test, the mysteries of Australia's new slow-bowling star Jack Iverson unravel in a rare run spree, which sees NSW pulverise the Victorian attack, including Iverson. Arthur Morris makes 182 and Keith Miller 83 in a better-than-even-time century stand.

Used at first change, Iverson takes three for 108 and is so disconsolate that he tells teammates he's thinking of 'giving it away: they've worked me out'. Miller admits later it was a deliberate assault on the late-blooming Victorian, playing only his 13th Sheffield Shield match at the age of 35.

JANUARY 1930

Don Bradman makes 452 not out, a new Australian first-class high, for NSW against Queensland and is chaired from the ground ... by his opponents.

DECEMBER 1910

Australia makes 6 for 494 at 100 runs an hour on the first day of the series against South Africa – a massive score still unequalled on any single day's Test play Down Under. The three sessions produce 147, 208 and 139 runs, Tests being scheduled over just five hours per day back then.

APRIL 1870

Australian captain-to-be Syd Gregory is born in the curator's cottage at the back of the ground. His father Ned was to play in the first official Test match seven years later.

Taber to Turner

Brian Taber His debut Test in Johannesburg was the first he ever attended. Figured in eight dismissals: Australia vs South Africa, December 1966.

Mike Tamblyn Brighton's Second XI captain famously told a 17-year-old Shane Warne to concentrate on his batting: Brighton Beach, Victoria, 1986.

The fella in the trilby hat The Melbourne spectator blamed by Arthur Mailey for the most expensive all-time analysis in Australia's first-class history: four for 362. 'The fella in the trilby hat kept dropping him. He dropped Jack Ryder six times,' he said: NSW vs Victoria, MCG, Christmas 1926. (Ryder made 295.)

Cec Thompson The first substitute fieldsman to take a Test catch for Australia at Brisbane's Exhibition Ground, December 1928.

George Thoms The post-war Victorian opener retired in his mid-20s to preserve his hands for his work as a gynaecologist and laser surgeon. Played one Test.

Henry Thornton Victoria's one-day cricketer of the year in his first season, 2021–22, he has five forenames – more than any Australian first-class cricketer since 1850. *Wisden* lists him as HTRJY Thornton, short for Henry Thomas Raphael James York Thornton. He answers most to his nickname: Horn. Is playing out of Adelaide now.

Three cheers for Lennie Having taken two remarkable reflex catches within half an hour to dismiss English masters Walter Hammond and Maurice Leyland, local hero Len Darling receives three rousing cheers from 85,000 ecstatic Melburnians at the MCG, January 1937.

Tom the Cheap Grocer One of Western Australian cricket's earliest and most generous philanthropists and sponsors, millionaire businessman Tom Wardle was directly responsible for many overseas champions being lured to the west in the '60s, the most imposing being heavyweight opening batsman Colin Milburn.

Ernie Toshack Paid a boy to sign a stack of official team autograph sheets on the HMAS *Strathaird* to England in 1948, only for the lad to mistakenly sign 'Toshak', forcing everyone to start afresh on a second set of sheets.

Dr Claude Tozer A decorated war hero and a gifted top-order batsman on the cusp of Australian selection, he was murdered by a jilted lover in December 1920. Only weeks earlier, opening the batting for an Australian XI against the touring English team, he scored 51 and 53 at the Gabba.

Sharon Tredrea The 1970s expresswoman was once rated by the legendary umpire Dickie Bird as being as fast as English Test bowler Paul Allott.

George Tribe A notable left-arm chinaman bowler selected three times by Australia in 1946, George had a sore shoulder one club Saturday and told his captain, North Melbourne's Bob Dempster, that he'd be unable to bowl.

North's most vocal supporter was a red-faced local abattoir worker, Rooster O'Connor, who loved George like a second son. 'Bob,' he kept yelling, 'put Tribe on.'

Dempster pleaded with Tribe. Unless he tried an over or two, Rooster would never shut up and when Tribe, still sore, bowled a succession of full tosses and long hops and conceded a dozen runs from his opening over, Rooster yelled again to Dempster, 'Take the imposter off and put Tribe on.'

Sam Trimble The pride of the far north coast of NSW, a 21-year-old Trimble was the first to score 1000 runs in Clunes and District cricket in 1955–56. His Bradman-like average was 271 and included seven hundreds, six not out. He was to become one of Queensland's finest and tour as reserve opener with Bobby Simpson's Australians to the West Indies in 1965.

Glenn Trimble also played for Australia, at white-ball level. He and his father Sam shared the same nickname: Munster.

Albert Trott The only cricketer to hit a ball over the famous Lord's Pavilion, in July 1899. The bowler was fellow Australian, MA (Monty) Noble.

John (Billy) Trumble Once bowled 19 maidens in a row: Melbourne, January 1886.

Victor Trumper Having been beaten by a sudden lifter from Victoria's Jack Saunders, Vic said, 'Why Jack, what a thing to do to an old friend. Well, it's either you or me for it.' An hour later, he was 100 not out. The incomparable batsman of the Golden Age, he scored Test cricket's first century before lunch at Old Trafford in

1902. His son, Vic junior, also represented NSW, as a bowler.

Another Victor Trumper Johnny Taylor.

Rod Tucker Bowls two overs in a row, after a rain interruption: Tasmania vs Queensland, Devonport, 1988–89.

Alan Turner Became the first Australian to hit a six to win a Test match. The bowler was Ewen Chatfield: Australia vs New Zealand, Auckland, 1976–77.

Turner & Ferris Australia's first great new-ball combination: CTB (Charlie) Turner and JJ (Jack) Ferris, 1886–90. On debut, they took 17 wickets in the first Ashes Test in Sydney, bowling through the first innings unchanged.

Twenty wickets in a match Lou Benaud, father of Richie and John, took 20 for 65 for Penrith Waratahs, Nepean B Grade, 1923–24.

TEST MATCH 'FIRSTS'

First ball faced
Charles Bannerman; Melbourne, 1877.

First to a double century
Billy Murdoch; Kennington Oval, London, 1884.

First to make four double centuries in the same calendar year
Michael Clarke, 2012.

First to 100 matches
Allan Border. He was bowled for a fifth ball blob – his first duck in six years. Melbourne, 1988.

First to 100 wickets
CTB (Terror) Turner in his 16th Test, in Sydney, 1895.

First substitute to take a catch
Billy Murdoch, fielding for England, dismissed teammate HJH (Tup) Scott at Lord's, 1884.

First to make 100 runs and take 10 wickets
Men: Alan Davidson against the West Indies, The Gabba, Brisbane, 1960.
Women: Betty Wilson against England, St Kilda, 1958.

First time floodlights used in a Test
Final session, first day, Australia vs New Zealand, WACA Ground, Perth, 1997.

TALL STORIES & TRUE

Mick Dowe, Skye CC's intrepid Fourth XI opener, sneaked down to his local indoor centre for some extra Friday night practice. One not out overnight, he had visions of a big one.

Programming the bowling machine to automatic, he went undismissed and at the end he casually asked how quick the machine could go.

'100 miles per hour, mate.'

'Good I'll try it,' he said. 'Crank it up.'

Retaking guard, he'd just lifted his bat when a full bunger hit him flush on his forearm. Within minutes his forearm was the size of a pumpkin. Thinking his arm was broken, he went to Frankston emergency and was released about midnight. Thankfully there was no break and he duly turned up the next day and even though he could hold his bat with just one hand, out he went to resume his knock, only to top-edge his first ball onto his chin. Back to hospital went Mick … for 11 stitches.

Returning right on stumps in thongs and shorts for some amber fluid therapy, he came across a 30 litre urn of boiling water in the kitchen. Wanting to do the right thing, he decided to empty it outside. On the way, one of the handles snapped and boiling water doused his bare feet, blistering his toes. 'It was 24 hours I don't want to have again,' he said. *2005.*

———

Bush scorebooks are traditionally poorly kept and error-ridden. When Nymagee played Grand in the Cobar Association, NSW, in 2002–03, the discrepancy in the two scorebooks was 40: 198 in one and 238 in the other. It was agreed that the two teams would split the difference and Grand's innings was 'set' at 218. In reply Nymagee was out for 217 and lost by a run.

... Tall stories & true continued

Having left the practice balls in his car at Rosny, Tasmania, Roger Woolley had the Clarence First XI warm up prematch at Kingston with apples and oranges originally intended for the afternoon tea. *1994–95.*

--- --- ---

In 1992, ABC commentator Neville Oliver said of the West Indian Junior Murray, 'If he has a child he'll have to become Junior Murray Senior.'

--- --- ---

Ken Young was on his way to 1000-plus runs for the 1987–88 season with new team Colts in the Chinchilla and District CA, Queensland, when local publican Greg Cadzow told him he'd shout his drinks for a whole week if he happened to score a century against his RSL-sponsored Club Hotel XI the following weekend.

'You're on,' said Ken.

Young played faultlessly without giving even a half chance, only at 92 to be dropped at short leg, a dolly of a catch to Don Clarke.

He scored his century and Cadzow duly sponsored his drinks for a week: not realising at the time that Clarke was one of Young's best mates!

--- --- ---

Rod McCurdy, the much-travelled 'rebel' paceman from Melbourne, was particularly lively this summer Saturday at Clarence, for Hobart first-grade cricket, 1980. Everyone was ducking and weaving and commending the Pup on his extreme pace. Later it was found the pitch was a yard short.

Tall stories & true continues overleaf ...

... Tall stories & true continued

Years ago, leading up to Bill Ponsford's eightieth birthday, I asked the old recordbreaker why he hadn't tried to match the feats of a young Don Bradman.

'I knew it was always hopeless trying to chase Bradman,' he said. 'He was ruthless.'

--- --- ---

Having badly smashed his ankle and unable to run between wickets, Mt Duneed's Ron Dodds was allowed to bat with a runner for more than a decade in Geelong's Southern District competition. He even won the Association's batting average in 1970–71.

--- --- ---

So superstitious was Queenslander Ken Mackay that he refused to have a Chapter 13 in his best-selling autobiography *Slasher Opens Up*, released in 1964.

--- --- ---

Touching a ball to unguarded fine leg, Ian Gribble ran four and was dismayed when the umpire signalled 'byes'. The bowler immediately appealed and, to Gribble's amazement, the umpire raised his finger. Geelong CA vs Cricket Club of India, Kardinia Park, 1961–62.

--- --- ---

Awarded a pack of vinyl records for being man of the match during an island match in the West Indies in 1955, Alan Davidson was still playing his favourite, by American swing king Glenn Miller, years afterwards.

... Tall stories & true continued

Cajoled into playing one last Prime Minister's XI game in 1959, Lindsay Hassett borrowed a bat from ex-teammate Arthur Morris. Having made a dozen or so, he was mobbed as he walked back into the pavilion at Manuka Oval and, on the spur of the moment, presented his bat to a young admirer.

'Lindsay, that was my favourite bat,' said Morris, aghast.

'But Arthur ... you should have seen the look on the boy's face.'

— — —

George Tribe once bowled a 14-ball over in a Shield match against Queensland after an umpire miscounted. 'Think I've had enough now,' said George, after the 14th.

— — —

Dollar's Laurie Thorsen was the long-time batting supremo in South Gippsland and this day was into his 80s when young Laurie Collins was introduced into the attack and told to 'bowl some rubbish'.

'He proceeded to bowl these ever-so-slow and ever-so-high full tosses,' said eyewitness Roy Bright. 'Higher and higher they went and Laurie almost turned himself inside out trying to whack 'em. He swiped at the first four or five and finally hit the sixth, straight to short point! I never saw so much effort for so little reward.'

— — —

Eight runs were awarded for hits over the fence in Sydney grade cricket in 1929–30.

Ugly to Urquhart

Ugly Australians In the days of no uniforms, ultralong hair, beards and much on-field misbehaviour, Ian Chappell and his Australian teams of the early 1970s were often pilloried. But they were also badly underpaid, received few concessions and hardly any outside support. During match week, it was left to Chappell to organise the taxis, team photos and a raft of other administrative matters.

Even into the mid-'80s, one Australian team manager was seen in suit pants, collar and tie hitting catches to the players on the morning of a Test in Adelaide.

Until the advent of World Series Cricket, the gatemen on major Sydney and Melbourne cricketing weekends received more money than the players. Little wonder Chappelli and co. rebelled.

Unaarrimin (Johnny Mullagh) The first great Indigenous batsman, he toured with the 1868 team to England. On his death, the day after his fiftieth birthday in 1891, he was described by the *Hamilton Spectator* as the 'WG Grace of Aboriginal cricketers'. The Johnny Mullagh Medal is presented each Melbourne Test to the man of the match.

Don Urquhart Selected only once by Queensland, but never played after monsoonal rains forced an abandonment of the Sheffield Shield match without a ball being bowled: Queensland vs Victoria, Brisbane, January 1971.

UMPIRING PEARLERS

Rodney Hogg was opening the bowling alongside Dennis Lillee in the 1981 New Year Test in Sydney against Sunil Gavaskar's Indians. Lillee was a huge advocate of shining the ball, Hogg not so. Rex Whitehead, on debut, was standing at Lillee's end and when the ball was returned to him for the third over of the match, Lillee looked in disgust at the ball and blasted Hogg for not keeping it in better nick.

Hogg bowled again and the ball came back to Lillee in even worse shape. Lillee blew up big-time and started swearing like a sailor.

'But I can't do it Dennis,' said Rod. 'I can't shine it.'

'Waddya mean, yer can't?'

'Because ... I'm wearing the wrong pants.'

Eye-witness Whitehead dined out on that one for years.

— — —

Len Pascoe induced what he thought was a huge edge in Perth one afternoon, only for umpire Dick French to rule 'not out'. Looking back down the wicket to slipsman and captain Greg Chappell, Pascoe said, 'Greg, do you mind taking the splinter out of the ball before you throw it back.'

— — —

In Adelaide during a Shield game, an in-form David Hookes was on his way to twin centuries and NSW wicketkeeper Steve Rixon settled over the stumps, with Pascoe struggling to maintain his pace. Len being Len, he immediately delivered some fruity curses directly back down the wicket, umpire Keith Butler telling him to settle down and never talk to a batsman again like that. 'The batsman? I was telling my bloody keeper to get back where he belongs,' said Pascoe.

... Umpiring pearlers continued

Mornington Peninsula umpire Ernie Hamid had given five lbs, all in the first hour of a match in 1977–78. At six for 41, Long Island's first match as a newly promoted District power was heading for an early finish. Ernie's eyesight and judgement were being seriously questioned.

As incoming batsman Wayne Ross walked in, Ernie said to him, 'Your boys aren't too happy with me, Rossy, are they?'

'I don't know why Ernie ... they were all absolutely plumb,' said Ross, with a wry smile. Not long into his innings Ross was rapped on his pads right in front, lost balance and ended up sprawled on the pitch. There was a huge shout; Ross thinking he too must also be out, lb.

'Fellas,' said Ernie. 'I've had enough of frivolous appeals: NOT OUT.'

Ross made 44 not out. Long Island recovered to nine for 155 and rolled Sorrento for 114.

— — —

Bruno Croatto was umpiring a Leongatha club game when he rejected a triumphant and prolonged 'that's gotta be out' lbw appeal from the bowler, Brian Gobbo. Incensed at the decision, Brian was carrying on, as can happen, when Croatto told him, 'Shut up, or I'll job you Gobbo.'

'That doesn't frighten me ... you'll never be able to catch me.'

'But you'll never be able to stop running either.'

— — —

Young Tony Ware had never umpired before, but out he was sent for a senior club game in Leongatha, Victoria, in the '60s. Koonwarra's Barry McGregor took the new cherry for the opening eight-ball over. After bowling 10, McGregor looked back at the umpire who maintained his position.

Umpiring pearlers continues overleaf ...

... Umpiring pearlers continued

He got to 13 and looked again. 'Surely that's got to be over,' he said.

'No,' said young Tony. 'You still have three and a half minutes of your eight-minute over to go!'

Ware was to become one of the Melbourne Cricket Ground's most able curators.

--- --- ---

George Price was umpiring a lightning premiership match at Korumburra, Victoria, in the late '60s when a batsman thundered a straight drive straight back at the bowler, Rob Fennell. The stumps at the non-striker's end were broken, with Ocka Elliott backing up and well out of his crease.

'I touched it. I touched it,' screamed Fennell.

To Ocka's disgust, George ceremoniously raised his finger.

'Did you see the ball deflect?' said Ocka. 'Surely there was no obvious deflection?'

'Rob said it hit his hand,' said George, 'and he would not tell me a lie. You're out.'

--- --- ---

Having taken a wicket in one of his opening overs, John (Spider) Morris, the tall speedster from Mulgrave, Victoria, immediately struck Mont Albert's Rick Barker low down on the front foot and bellowed an appeal. It was plumb: missing off, missing leg, catapulting the middle. He was sure he had two from two.

'Not out,' said the umpire.

'You're kiddin' me! Why?'

'Too much seam, heading down leg.'

Next ball, Rick's middle stump cartwheeled almost back to the keeper.

'Christ,' said Spider, 'that one must have been close. Just missed a hat-trick!'

... Umpiring pearlers continued

At Orange, NSW, one day, the rostered umpire refused to uphold even one appeal. Afterwards over a drink, one of the aggrieved locals asked him where his dog was.

'What dog? I haven't got a dog.'

'Well, you're the first blind bloke we've struck without one.'

Grafton, NSW, legend Henry Ellem was gaining prodigious turn this day with his left-arm spinners, impressing everyone including the veteran umpire. 'Wish I'd brought my spectacles,' he said. 'I'd have liked a really good look at this stuff.'

Cricket's new glamour boy Don Bradman is controversially given out lbw for a sixth-ball duck in an exhibition match in West Maitland, April 1929. 'If he was Jesus Christ himself,' said umpire Peter Bailey, 'I'd have still given him out.' Bradman later wrote that the ball would have missed his leg stump by a foot.

A bush batsman was hit plumb in front and there was a loud, unanimous appeal. 'Not out,' said the umpire and a leg bye run was recorded. On reaching the other end, the lucky batsman said to the umpire, 'Gee, I thought I was a goner.'

'So you bloody well would have been,' came the reply, 'if you were a member of the visiting team.'

The touring English were playing a bush international against a Victorian Country XI in 1928–29 when Douglas Jardine middled a forcing shot straight at square leg umpire Ross Freeman. Having only just retired from playing, Freeman pocketed the reflex catch. He was suspended for two weeks.

van Vugt to Voges

Geoffrey van Vugt Once hit one of my leggies over the small scoreboard and almost into the old soap factory at Port Melbourne, in the late '80s. I told him it was a bloody slog and Vic Aanensen at slip said, 'Hang on a minute, Guru. Have a look to see where it has gone!' It was huge.

Tom Veivers Bowled 95.1 overs in an innings at Old Trafford in July 1964, a record by an Australian in Tests.

'It was cool and a huge wind was blowing, making it hard for the faster bowlers,' he said. 'Simmo [Bob Simpson] said, "Tommy, I think you'd better bowl the first over today." First ball, Ken Barrington edged between the keeper Wally Grout and Simmo … and Simmo told me to continue. He kept me going and going … and going!' (Barrington made 256. Veivers' figures were 95.1–37–155–3.)

Syd Vellnagel 'The Bradman of Brigalow' amassed 1997 runs (with 10 hundreds) and 189 wickets (with two hat-tricks): Chinchilla and District CA, Queensland, 1946–47.

Gordon Vidler Australia's premier collector of cricketana in the immediate post-war years. He possessed thousands of books, rare magazines, photographs, Bradman ephemera, brochures, catalogues, tour guides, cigarette and trade cards, posters and scrapbooks, all spread throughout his house in Spring Hill, in the Northern Rivers region of NSW.

Adam Voges The oldest cricketer, at 35, to score a Test century on debut: Roseau, Dominica, West Indies, 2015. Remains among an elite few to average 60-plus in Tests.

Waldron to Wright

Terry Waldron Captained 16 of a record 21 'bush internationals' against overseas touring teams. A batsman–wicketkeeper, he played against all countries, bar South Africa. Later was a prominent, accessible Parliamentarian.

Syd Walford Senior Captained NSW in his only interstate game in Australia: NSW vs Queensland, Brisbane Exhibition Ground, April 1893.

Alan Walker Produced the extraordinary match figures of 14 for 14 in a Sydney grade match in 1946–47. Representing Manly against Cumberland, he took seven for eight and seven for six. Later he toured with the 1949–50 Australians, without playing a Test. Also an Australian Wallaby, he scored one of the great rugby tries at Twickenham.

Charlie Walker The only Australian Ashes tourist to go on multiple tours (1930 and 1938) without playing even one Test.

Max Walker So successful was he as a raconteur and author in retirement that, for a time, he was Australia's best-selling author, with *How to Hypnotise Chooks and Other Great Yarns* and *How to Kiss a Crocodile* all written with a favourite fountain pen in impeccable long hand.

Tim Wall The first to take 10 wickets in a Sheffield Shield innings, in Sydney, 1932–33. Don Bradman rated him as the best new-ball bowler of his time.

Mike Walsh The first Victorian scorer to tally 1500 matches, across all levels, including Australian touring

teams from 1987–2002. His service to Essendon CC started in 1963–64 and continued into 2022–23. At Premier First XI level alone, he has scored more than 700 matches.

Doug Walters The Maitland junior produced match figures of nine for four and eight for seven in the Newcastle Christmas competition at Robins Oval, 1959. Later became one of the most idolised Test cricketers of the mid-'60s and '70s.

During a stint in National Service, his army mates dubbed him 'Hanoi': they reckoned he was always bombed at night.

Ben Wardill The doyen of early cricket secretaries, the Melbourne Cricket Club's membership increased tenfold during his three decades in control. He also managed three Australian touring teams to England, including the MCC-backed 1886 side.

Shane Warne The most inspired Australian selection of them all. When first chosen for an Australian B team that toured Zimbabwe in 1991, his first-class career record was one wicket, average 102, strike rate 222. He lost 19 kilograms in 1992 leading into the senior tour of Sri Lanka, where he soon established himself as a spin bowler with rare gifts. Is now rated, alongside Don Bradman, as the finest Australian cricketer of all and, ahead of the Don, as its ultimate celebrity.

His 2018 autobiography *No Spin* sold a near-record 54,000 copies. On his death, aged 52, in 2022, his personal fortune was estimated at $50 million plus.

In retirement he played professional poker and a lot of golf, once having a hole-in-one at the famous 16th at Augusta National.

Warne was at one time engaged to the Hollywood actress Elizabeth Hurley.

Warnie's nicknames included Twistie, Showbags, Hollywood, Young Barks, Truman, Elvis, The Sheik of Tweak, Suicide, Jaws, Warnie and The King.

Tommy Warne No relation to Shane, he also bowled leg-breaks. A testimonial match at the MCG in 1911 raised £234 despite inclement weather. Once made 402 in a Melbourne First XI club match.

Was curator at Carlton's leafy Princes Park, from 1898–1943.

David Warner Represented Australia even before he'd played first-class cricket for NSW.

Daniel Warwick Midway through a new Mornington Peninsula A grade record of 305 not out, he broke his favourite bat, but refused to change it and kept finding the middle, in all hitting 21 sixes and 20 fours: Baxter vs Somerville, Baxter Park, October 2007. Somerville's captain Mal Coutts said, 'No matter where we bowled he just smashed it. I needed 25 fielders.'

John Watkins Overcome by paralysing stage-fright, Watkins bowled a series of the widest wides in memory during his one-off Test: Sydney, 1972–73.

Graeme Watson Struck flush on the nose by an accidental beamer from Tony Greig in 1971–72, he was on the critical list in a Melbourne hospital for a week, having 20 litres of blood transfusions.

Len Watt The first to broadcast a cricket match in Australia: the Charles Bannerman Testimonial at the Sydney Cricket Ground in 1922.

Mark Waugh His soaring six against Daniel Vettori landed on the roof of the five-storey Lillee–Marsh Stand and was later measured to be 130 yards (almost 120 metres): Australia vs NZ, WACA Ground, Perth, November 1997.

Steve Waugh Once hit this writer for 32 runs from a six-ball over: Thames Valley Gents vs The Australian Crusaders, Teddington, Hampton Court, UK, June 1987. It was a like a tennis match: 646466.

Dirk Wellham The first to captain three states in Sheffield Shield matches.

Kepler Wessels The only cricketer to represent both Australia and South Africa in Tests.

Dav Whatmore Took guard in a pool of blood after fellow debutant, Victoria's number three Doug Rolfe, turned his back on a bouncer from Western Australia's Dennis Lillee, was struck in the back of the head and carried from the ground in Melbourne, March 1976.

Les Wheeler Told he would be lucky to walk again, having contracted polio in the early '50s in Gippsland, Les refused to stop keeping wickets, initially using a walking stick to help him from end to end. The callipers on his right leg stretched from his foot to his hip, yet he still played for 35 more years and scored 10 centuries for Toora and one for Korumburra.

Turning to umpiring, in one game he joined in an appeal with all the players. 'Everyone looked at me in amazement,' he said, 'before we all broke up laughing.'

Arthur E Whitelaw The Melbourne-born soap magnate gifted Don Bradman a thousand pounds after he witnessed the young Don make a triple century at Headingley in 1930. The gift was almost double each player's tour fee.

'It would have been nice if Don had put even 50 pounds on the bar for us that night,' said Vic Richardson, 'but he never did. We were in there waiting for him and he waltzed past us saying he was tired and would have supper in his room.'

RS (Dick) Whitington Campaigned unsuccessfully for the five Victory tests in England in 1945 to be accorded official status. He'd opened for the Australian Services XI in each of the matches, the games beginning less than a fortnight after the end of World War II in Europe.

A high-profile journalist and cricket author, Whitington 'ghosted' six of Keith Miller's books, one a year, from *Cricket Caravan* (1950) to *Cricket Typhoon* (1955). Among those who contributed forewords to the books there were an eminent musician, a high commissioner and an Australian prime minister. Few possessed a more impressive A-list of contacts than Keith and Dick.

W

Mike Whitney A number 11 in almost any team, Whit blocked out a final maiden over from champion Kiwi Richard Hadlee to save a Test match for Australia in Melbourne, December 1987. He worked in TV in retirement and as one of the funniest after-dinner speakers.

PL Williams Schoolboy coach and mentor to Test quartet Lindsay Hassett, Ross Gregory, Ian Johnson and Sam Loxton in the 1930s.

Betty Wilson Affable, generous and known to her extended family as Aunt Bette, Australia's champion post-war women's cricketer liked to save on heating bills by making her own draught excluders and packing them with 50 cent coins. 'There was a small fortune there when it came to clean up her house,' said her nephew Ken Wilson.

Paul (Blocker) Wilson Failed to take a wicket or make a run in his only Test: Australia vs India, Eden Gardens, Kolkata, 1997–98.

Edward Windsor The pre-eminent early Launceston cricketer, he represented the north of Tasmania almost 50 times and won an invitation to play in Monty Noble's Testimonial match in Sydney in 1908, scoring 78 from number 10 and sharing a 225-run partnership with Warwick Armstrong.

Wingello Oval The slopiest ground in the Southern Highlands of NSW, famous for Bill O'Reilly's first-ball dismissal of Don Bradman on day two of a game in

January 1926, after the young Don had made a double century on the first day of the match at Bowral.

George Wintle The General Manager of South Sydney Junior Leagues Club orchestrated the biggest club recruiting coup in history when Wes Hall captained Randwick in the 1965–66 Sydney grade season.

The celebrated West Indian express bowler took a Sydney-high 56 first-grade wickets and lifted Randwick into the semifinals. Every expense was paid and a handsome salary provided for five months of coaching.

Luke Wintle At the front oval at St Bede's one memorable Saturday in 2010, he powered a straight drive over the three-storey, 20 metre-high Brothers' apartments and into the carpark of the nearby Mentone RSL in Palermo Street. It took 10 minutes to retrieve it, the monster hit being estimated at 125 metres. I had the best seat in the house, at the non-striker's end.

Barry Wood At Randwick in 1965–66, he stood over the stumps to West Indian express bowler Wes Hall … and lived.

Bill Woodfull Rejected a knighthood for his sporting achievements, in 1934. Was to work for 46 years as a schoolteacher, principal and educationalist. At Melbourne High, he mentored a young Keith Miller.

Resigned as captain after Australia's humiliating loss in the first Bodyline Test, an offer accepted by the selectors. But when he told them he would also no longer continue as a player, he was immediately reinstated and played all five Tests.

The first to twice carry his bat in Tests, he was known as The Great Unbowlable.

John Woods Among the few to play 500 consecutive matches, without missing even one Saturday. All of his 509 games, spread over four decades from 1978–79 to 2015–16, were on hard wickets for Mt Eliza's lower XIs on the Mornington Peninsula. Kennilworth's Ron Halliday was another to play 500 in a row leading into the new millennium.

Sammy Woods The first bowler to take seven wickets with seven balls, for Royston College, Sydney, 1882–83. He later played Test cricket for both Australia and England.

Harry Wren The southern Riverina's master batsman, Harry was in good form this day for his local Meat Works XI and started to chide his opponent, Narrandera fast bowler George Haff, boasting that he could play him with a candle. Next ball his leg stump cascaded almost all the way back to the keeper. The roar of delight from Haff and co. was long, loud and unanimous.

The Wrigglesworths of Bundalaguah Four generations of Wrigglesworths have represented Bundalaguah CC most Saturdays since the club's inception in 1921. Ian Wrigglesworth played for Victoria and his son, Tom, is a promising prospect at Wesley College. What was once a matting wicket, on a rough corner of the family's farm, is now one of the pride-and-joy turf grounds in Gippsland, with its own expansive indoor centre: a veritable paradise for cricketers of all ages. A second ground has also been developed.

The club held its centenary dinner in 2021 with many a Wrigglesworth present. And for the first time, in autumn 2022, a wedding was held in the club's indoor centre. 'It was one of those old-fashioned country weddings,' said 83-year-old Neil Wrigglesworth. 'We had seats all around all decked out in white linen. There was a caterer and four boxes of grog. It was help yourself.'

Neil and wife Marion are among six Wrigglesworth family members to be 'Bundy' life members. They live next door to the ground, also noted for its giant eucalypt, estimated to be at least 400 years old.

Ian (Lefty) Wright Played in 15 First XI premierships in Warrnambool, a feat matched later by Trevor McKenzie from another far-west Victorian club, Nestles. 'I actually caught Lefty in the early '90s and thought I had a few good years left,' said McKenzie, 'only for us to lose six Grand Finals in a row. It was a record not meant to be broken.'

WACA HAPPENINGS

NOVEMBER 2016

'Spidercam', the large and very heavy roving aerial camera, crashes with force into the sightscreen after a wire snaps on the fifth day of the Australia vs South Africa match, over 109. Technicians held up play and retrieved the camera. 'It was very noisy and mildly scary too,' says eyewitness Mark Browning.

NOVEMBER 1998

Jason Gillespie takes four wickets in six balls in the second Ashes Test. His analysis: W•WW1W.

NOVEMBER 1971

Peter Bedford, the VFL Brownlow Medallist who loved cricket more than footy, was batting against a 22-year-old Dennis Lillee on a grassy, typically bouncy Perth wicket. Only two years earlier, 'Wheels' had made a career-best 134 not out in Melbourne against Lillee and co.

'But he got me back this day,' he said. 'Dennis was bowling with the Freo doctor behind him. The pitch was grassy and the ball was flying around. We were trying to avoid the outright and I nicked one through the hands of third slip. Dennis was ropeable. As I was running up the wicket, I just slightly brushed him. Foolishly, I came back for two and DK dipped his shoulder into me on the way past, but I had enough momentum to stay on my feet and make my crease.

'DK threw his marker back an extra five yards and I needed binoculars to see him, he was that far back. This one is going to be quick, I thought. Get ready to duck. As he was launching, I was already on my foot waiting for the short one.

... WACA happenings continued

To my surprise it was a half volley. I came forward looking to defend, but the ball was so fast the bat wobbled in my hand and the ball trickled onto the off stump and dislodged the off bail.

'We saved the game and DK came straight into the rooms afterwards, apologising about the hip and shoulder. Coming from Port Melbourne, it didn't bother me. "That's okay, Den," I said.

"'And Wheels, that ball to you ... " he said, "it's the fastest I've ever bowled.'"

DECEMBER 1970

Just as Ashes debutant Greg Chappell is on the verge of an entrancing, imperious century on debut, the ABC in the Eastern states crosses to the regular seven o'clock Sunday night news bulletin and misses the great moment. It was the first of Chappell's 24 Test centuries.

Don Bradman, cricket's ultimate batsman, scorer of an Australian-record 212 centuries.

Leg-spinning legend Hugh Chilvers was still playing at Sydney first grade level into his mid-fifties. The only representative tour he was chosen for, to NZ in 1933–34 with an Australian B team, was cancelled.

Darrel Baldock, the teenage cricket star.

Baldock family archives

White-ball specialist Aaron Finch in his favourite junior footy gear.

Nelma Grout, Wally's daughter, umpired at Brisbane first-grade level.

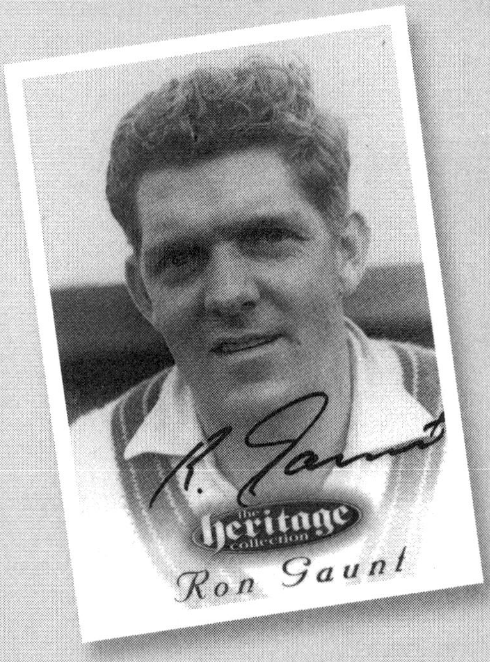

Ron Gaunt took a wicket in his first, extended, over of Test cricket.

Ian Johnson bowled without socks in his first post-war Tests.

Late '70s Victorian paceman John Leehane had one of the great nicknames: Luna ... short for 'lunatic'.

Brendon Julian was a notable Test fast bowler before becoming the face of Fox Sports cricket.

Stephen Laffer/*Australian Cricket* magazine

Young Sam Loxton was always going to be a cricketer. His father, Sam senior, and mother Annie were Prahran CC stalwarts, also running the local electrical shop adjacent to Toorak Park.

Arthur Mailey remained a big name in Australian cricket, long after his playing retirement, as an irreverent critic and a cartoonist.

A teenage Ken Mackay made a triple century and took 10 wickets in an innings in the same schoolboy's match in Brisbane on the eve of World War II.

Ashley Mallett was once hit for five sixes in a row by the South African Mike Procter.

Graham McKenzie's strapping physique triggered his nickname of 'Garth' after the ageless comic strip hero.

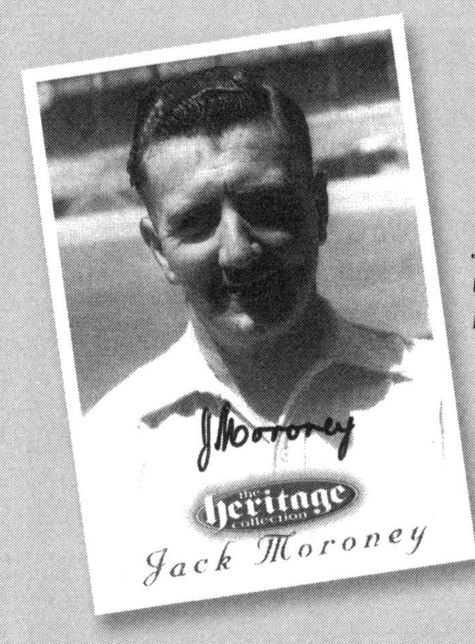

Jack Moroney made a pair in his only Test against England in 1950–51.

Lisle Nagel parted his hair in a different way to his identical brother Vernon so teammates knew who was who.

Len Pascoe was fast and fiery, and occasionally late home ...

Richie Robinson, a wicketkeeper and a natural number seven, opened the batting in his only Tests for Australia, in 1977.

'One-Test wonder' Dawn Rae (right) and her opening partner Jan Wilkinson shared a record 478-run stand in A grade Melbourne club cricket in the mid-'70s.

The Bundalaguah CC life members' board currently includes six Wrigglesworths, with more to come ...

X

Xavier

Xavier College One of Melbourne's prestigious private schools with a most distinguished set of old boys. Its highest profile sportsman was a libertine, the maverick chinaman bowler Leslie O'Brien (Chuck) Fleetwood-Smith – cricketer, womaniser, gambler and drinker – and he was only 16.

Originally from Stawell before the family's move to inner Melbourne, Chuck boarded at Xavier for seven and a half years, from 1917 when he was nine. His wild ways saw him expelled 'on a delicate issue', probably involving a girl, late in 1924.

He'd played alongside boy wonder Karl Schneider in back-to-back Xavier Associated Public Schools premierships in 1923 and 1924. The team was rarely beaten in their time.

Chuck was to become one of Victoria's foremost and most loved sportsmen and, in 1937 in Adelaide, he helped Australia win a Test match when he bowled Walter Hammond with an unplayable back-break. He sank to his knees and said to his captain Don Bradman, 'Is that what you wanted, Don?'

His biographer Greg Growden rated Chuck as 'the greatest pantsman in the history of Australian cricket'. He called his book *A Wayward Genius*.

Chuck ended up a vagrant, sleeping under the stars beneath a Melbourne city bridge on the Yarra.

Yabba to Youngest

Yabba Cricket's peerless barracker Stephen Harold Gascoigne has a permanent presence thanks to a bronze statue in his honour residing in the front rows in the old 'Hill' area at the Sydney Cricket Ground. Known for his sharp wit and caustic heckling, he once told Douglas Jardine to 'leave our flies alone. They're the only friends you've got,' he said.

Away from the SCG, Yabba worked as a rabbit-oh.

Dennis Yagmich As a teenager, he was asked by his Swan Valley vineyard neighbours if he'd like to keep wickets in their backyard tests. He and childhood mate Tony Mann were to later play at representative levels, Mann making a century as a nightwatchman for Australia.

Graham Yallop The first to wear a full helmet and visor in a Test match, in the Caribbean in 1978.

Bob Young Made seven ducks in his first seven innings with Koorooman juniors: Leongatha & District, Victoria, late 1940s.

Ian Young Father of one-Test allrounder Shaun Young, he acted as secretary, coach and curator at South Launceston from the mid-'80s.

Youngest Sydney grade captain Ollie Davies of Manly–Warringah, aged 18 years and 118 days, vs Randwick Petersham, February 2019. As the Australian Under 19 captain, he was, in effect, the third choice, with Jay Lenton part of the Big Bash and Cameron Merchant unavailable because of his involvement in Channel Nine's *Married At First Sight*.

Zadow to Zoehrer

Bob Zadow Having scored 900 runs at an average of 90 for Kirby's Hotel XI on matting wickets against two-piece balls at Katherine, NT, in 1978, he soon became a South Australian regular.

Frank Zanelli Scorer of nine centuries in one unforgettable late 1930s season, he led Nagambie, Victoria, to 18 Seymour and District CA premierships. His CV also includes a 381-run partnership, a golfing handicap of near scratch, state lawn bowls representation and four Nagambie football premierships.

Andrew Zesers The youngest to 100 first-class wickets, a feat he achieved before his 21st birthday. Was a reserve member of Australia's victorious 1987 World Cup ODI team.

Keith Ziebell Queensland's number five amassed the highest score, 212 not out, of any Australian cricketer with a surname starting with Z: Melbourne, December 1966. He was dropped five times. All the Victorians bowled, bar wicketkeeper Ray Jordon.

Alf Ziehike The first Hornsby district batsman to amass five centuries in the same season: northern Sydney, 1939–40.

Tony Zimbulus The first cricketer of Greek descent to play at first-class level. Once dismissed Don Bradman, in Perth in 1938.

Herb Zischke 'The Bradman of the Lockyer' scored a double and six single centuries on his way to a season average of 238, in 1947–48. A farmer from Hatton Vale, Queensland, he had only a brief flirtation with cricket in the Big Smoke.

Tim Zoehrer An ebullient and polarising personality, he was rated by Ashley Mallett as the most exciting wrist-spinning prospect in all Australasia, after he unbuckled his wicketkeeping pads and took a 'five-for' against South Australia. 'He has more natural ability as a leg spinner than any I have seen on the first-class scene for many years,' wrote Mallett in *Cricketer* magazine. 'I have seen Shane Warne in the nets. And right now Tim is the one to write home about.'

Reserve wicketkeeper on Australia's 1993 Ashes tour, Zoehrer topped the first-class touring averages, ahead of Warne, only to fall out with national coach Bob Simpson. He played the last of his 10 Tests in 1987.

Stumps

Author Ken Piesse still has time for weekend cricket at Mount Eliza CC on Saturdays and the Australian Cricket Society on Sundays. He played his best cricket in his early thirties at Port Melbourne CC in the 1980s, and still regards his old Borough teammates as brothers.

Peter Glenton

PREVIOUS CRICKET BOOKS BY
KEN PIESSE
FOR ECHO PUBLISHING

2010: *Great Australian Cricket Stories*

2012: *Dynamic Duos, Cricket's Finest Pairs and Partnerships*

2013: *Great Ashes Moments*

2014: *Favourite Cricket Yarns*
(updated in 2020)

2017: *A Pictorial History of Australian Cricket*

echo

Echo Publishing
An imprint of Bonnier Books UK
4th Floor, Victoria House, Bloomsbury Square
London WC1B 4DA
www.echopublishing.com.au
www.bonnierbooks.co.uk

Echo Publishing acknowledges the traditional custodians of Country throughout Australia. We recognise their continuing connection to land, sea and waters. We pay our respects to Elders past and present.

First Nations peoples are advised that this book contains images and names of deceased people.

First published 2022

Printed and bound in Australia by Griffin Press

The paper this book is printed on is certified against the Forest Stewardship Council® Standards. Griffin Press holds FSC® chain of custody certification SGS-COC-005088. FSC® promotes environmentally responsible, socially beneficial and economically viable management of the world's forests.

Cover design and internal concept by Design by Committee
Page layout by transformer.com.au
Edited by Melody Lord

All photographs in this book are the property of Ken Piesse, unless otherwise attributed.
Front cover. Clockwise from top: Steve Smith (Gregg Porteous/Newspix); Dennis Lillee (Ken Piesse archive); Merv Hughes (News Ltd/Newspix); Adam Gilchrist (News Ltd/Newspix).
Back cover. Clockwise from top: Scott Boland (Neb, Creative Commons <creative commons.org/licenses/by-sa/4.0/deed.en>, image deep-etched); Don Bradman (Ken Piesse archive, golf club added by designer); Richie Benaud (Creative Commons, public domain); Shane Warne (Patrick Eagar/Ken Piesse collection/*Australian Cricket* magazine).

A catalogue entry for this book is available from the National Library of Australia

ISBN: 9781760687502 (paperback)

ISBN: 9781760687519 (ebook)

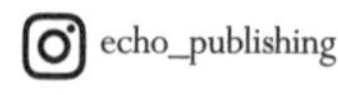 echo_publishing

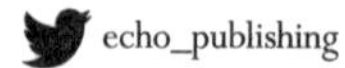 echo_publishing

 echopublishingaustralia